TREADING WATER IN AN EMPTY POOL

TREADING WATER IN AN EMPTY POOL

REALLIFE**STUFF**FOR**MEN** ON DISAPPOINTMENT

A BIBLE DISCUSSION GUIDE FEATURING

NAVPRESS®

BRINGING TRUTH TO LIFE

OUR GUARANTEE TO YOU

We believe so strongly in the message of our books that we are making this quality guarantee to you. If for any reason you are disappointed with the content of this book, return the title page to us with your name and address and we will refund to you the list price of the book. To help us serve you better, please briefly describe why you were disappointed. Mail your refund request to: NavPress, P.O. Box 35002, Colorado Springs, CO 80935.

The Navigators is an international Christian organization. Our mission is to reach, disciple, and equip people to know Christ and to make Him known through successive generations. We envision multitudes of diverse people in the United States and every other nation who have a passionate love for Christ, live a lifestyle of sharing Christ's love, and multiply spiritual laborers among those without Christ.

NavPress is the publishing ministry of The Navigators. NavPress publications help believers learn biblical truth and apply what they learn to their lives and ministries. Our mission is to stimulate spiritual formation among our readers.

Cover design by Arvid Wallen
Cover illustration by Jared Lee
Creative Team: Steve Parolini, Jim Lund, Cara Iverson, Pat Miller

Written and compiled by Steve Parolini

Some of the anecdotal illustrations in this book are true to life and are included with the permission of the persons involved. All other illustrations are composites of real situations, and any resemblance to people living or dead is coincidental.

Unless otherwise identified, all Scripture quotations in this publication are taken from *THE MESSAGE* (MSG). Copyright © 1993, 1994, 1995, 1996, 2000, 2001, 2002. Used by permission of NavPress Publishing Group.

Printed in Canada

2 3 4 5 6 7 8 9 10 11 / 10 09 08 07 06

FOR A FREE CATALOG OF NAVPRESS BOOKS & BIBLE STUDIES,
CALL 1-800-366-7788 (USA) OR 1-800-839-4769 (CANADA)

CONTENTS

ABOUT THE
REALLIFESTUFFFORMEN
SERIES

Let your love dictate how you deal with me;
　　teach me from your textbook on life.
I'm your servant—help me understand what that means,
　　the inner meaning of your instructions. . . .
Break open your words, let the light shine out,
　　let ordinary people see the meaning.

—PSALM 119:124-125,130

We're all yearning for understanding—for truth, wisdom, and hope. Whether we suffer in the simmering quiet of uncertainty or the megaphone cacophony of disbelief, we long for a better life—a more meaningful existence. We want to be Men Who Matter. But the fog of "real life stuff" we encounter every day obscures the life we crave, so we go on with the way things are.

Sometimes we pretend we don't care.

We do.

Sometimes we pretend everything is fine.

It isn't.

The truth is, the real life stuff matters. In that fog, there are things about our wives, our children, our friends, our work, and, most significantly, ourselves that cause varying degrees of distress, discomfort, and disease.

The REAL LIFE STUFF FOR MEN series is a safe place for exploring the truth about that fog. But it's not a typical Bible study. You won't find any fill-in-the-blank questions in these pages. Nor will you find any pat answers. It's likely you'll come away with more questions rather than fewer. But through personal reflection and—in a small group—lively discussion (the best part of a Bible study anyway), these books will take you where you *need* to go and bring greater hope and meaning to your life.

Each of the books in this series provides a place to ask the hard questions of yourself and others, a place to find comfort in the chaos, a place to enlarge understanding, and—with the guidance of the Holy Spirit—a place to discover Real Life Hope that brings meaning to the everyday.

INTRODUCTION

I hate life. As far as I can see, what happens on earth is a bad business. It's smoke—and spitting into the wind.

—Ecclesiastes 2:17

Unlike the animals, who seem quite content to simply be themselves, we humans are always looking for ways to be more than or other than what we find ourselves to be. We explore the countryside for excitement, search our souls for meaning, shop the world for pleasure. We try this. Then we try that. The usual fields of endeavor are money, sex, power, adventure, and knowledge.

Everything we try is so promising at first! But nothing ever seems to amount to very much. We intensify our efforts—but the harder we work at it, the less we get out of it. Some people give up early and settle for a humdrum life. Others never seem to learn, and so they flail away through a lifetime, becoming less and less human by the year, until by the time they die there is hardly enough humanity left to compose a corpse.

Ecclesiastes is a famous—maybe the world's most famous—witness to this experience of futility. The acerbic wit catches our attention. The stark honesty compels notice. And people do notice—oh, how they notice! Nonreligious and religious alike notice. Unbelievers and believers notice. More than a few of them are surprised to find this kind of thing in the Bible.

But it is most emphatically and necessarily in the Bible in order to call a halt to our various and futile attempts to make something of our lives, so that we can give our full attention to God—who God is and what he does to make something of us. Ecclesiastes actually doesn't say that much about God; the author leaves that to the other sixty-five books of the Bible. His task is to expose our total incapacity to find the meaning and completion of our lives on our own.

—FROM THE INTRODUCTION TO ECCLESIASTES, *THE MESSAGE*

If we are honest with ourselves, we must admit the reality of seasons when life seems nothing more than "smoke and spitting into the wind." Perhaps those seasons are fleeting, a random thought or a moment of disappointment; maybe they come and go as hurricanes or tornadoes; or perhaps they linger casually beneath the surface of the everyday, silent to everyone but you. But they do exist, and like determined termites, they gnaw at the core of who we, as men, want to be.

It may be reasonable to admit intellectually that we can't fully know life's meaning on our own—that only God can "make something of us." But it's nigh impossible to live that truth out when the drone of meaninglessness permeates our reality. "Is that all there is?" becomes the weary battle cry of many men. It takes shape in the spoken and unspoken: "I hate my job," "My wife doesn't look like the person I married," "I don't know how to have fun anymore," "I am trapped in mundania." Like the protagonist of Ecclesiastes, we slowly or suddenly realize the futility of life. We feel like we're treading water in an empty pool.

And then we can't get out.

No amount of prodding, encouragement, or "I think I can" self-talk can move us. And that brings us to this study. We begin by acknowledging how deeply we are stuck. Then, with a community of fellow travelers huddled together in a scrum, we can move gradually, methodically, and intentionally forward—led on by the truth of God's role in all of this.

Life is much more than smoke and spitting into the wind. We instinctively know that. Yet it's in the slogging that this truth becomes palpable.

Slog on.

HOW TO USE THIS DISCUSSION GUIDE

This discussion guide is meant to be completed on your own and in a small group. So before you begin, line up a discussion group. Perhaps you already participate in a men's group. That works. Maybe you know a few friends who could do coffee once a week. That works, too. Ask around. You'll be surprised how many of your coworkers, team members, and neighbors would be interested in a small-group study—especially a study like this that doesn't require vast biblical knowledge. A group of four to six is optimal—any bigger and one or more members will likely be shut out of discussions. Your small group can also be two. Choose a friend who isn't afraid to "tell it like it is." Make sure each person has his own copy of the book.

1. *Read* the Scripture passages and other readings in each lesson on your own. Let it all soak in. Then use the white space provided to "think out loud on paper." Note content in the readings that troubles you, inspires you, confuses you, or challenges you. Be honest. Be bold. Don't shy away from the hard things. If you don't understand the passage, say so. If you don't agree, say that, too. You may choose to go over the material in one thirty- to forty-five-minute focused session. Or perhaps you'll spend twenty minutes a day on the readings.

2. *Think* about what you read. Think about what you wrote. Always ask, "What does this mean?" and "Why does this matter?" about

the readings. Compare different Bible translations. Respond to the questions we've provided. You may have a lot to say on one topic, little on another. That's okay. Come back to this when you're in your small group. Allow the experience of others to broaden your wisdom. You'll be stretched here—called upon to evaluate what you've discovered and asked to make practical sense of it. In community, that stretching can often be painful and sometimes even embarrassing. But your willingness to be transparent—your openness to the possibility of personal growth—will reap great rewards.

3. *Pray* as you go through the entire session: before you read a word, in the middle of your thinking process, when you get stuck on a concept or passage, and as you approach the time when you'll explore these passages and thoughts together in a small group. Pause when you need to ask God for inspiration or when you need to cry out in frustration. Speak your prayers, be silent, or use the prayer starter we've provided and write a prayer at the bottom of each page.

4. *Live.* (That's "live" as in "rhymes with give" as in "Give me something I can really use in my life.") Before you meet with your small group, complete as much of this section as you can (particularly the "What I Want to Discuss" section). Then, in your small group, ask the hard questions about what the lesson means to you. Dig deep for relevant, reachable goals. Record your real-world plan in the book. Commit to following through on these plans, and prepare to be held accountable.

5. *Follow up.* Don't let the life application drift away without action. Be accountable to small-group members and refer to previous "Live" as in "rhymes with give" sections often. Take time at the beginning of each new study to review. See how you're doing.

6. *Repeat* as necessary.

SMALL-GROUP STUDY TIPS

After going through each week's study on your own, it's time to sit down with others and go deeper. Here are a few thoughts on how to make the most of your small-group discussion time.

Set ground rules. You don't need many. Here are two:

First, you'll want group members to make a commitment to the entire eight-week study. A binding legal document with notarized signatures and commitments written in blood probably isn't necessary, but you know your friends best. Just remember this: Significant personal growth happens when group members spend enough time together to really get to know each other. Hit-and-miss attendance rarely allows this to occur.

Second, agree together that everyone's story is important. Time is a valuable commodity, so if you have an hour to spend together, do your best to give each person ample time to express concerns, pass along insights, and generally feel like a participating member of the group. Small-group discussions are not monologues. However, a one-person-dominated discussion isn't always a bad thing. Not only is your role in a small group to explore and expand your own understanding, it's also to support one another. If someone truly needs more of the floor, give it to him. There will be times when the needs of the one outweigh the needs of the many. Use good judgment and allow extra space when needed. *Your* time might be next week.

Meet regularly. Choose a time and place, and stick to it. No one likes showing up to Coffee Cupboard at 6:00 AM, only to discover the meeting was moved to Breakfast Barn at seven. Consistency removes stress that could otherwise frustrate discussion and subsequent personal growth. It's only eight weeks. You can do this.

Talk openly. If you enter this study with shields up, you're probably not alone. And you're not a "bad person" for your hesitation to unpack your life in front of friends or strangers. Maybe you're skeptical about the value of revealing the deepest parts of who you are to others. Maybe you're simply too afraid of what might fall out of the suitcase. You don't have to go to a place where you're uncomfortable. If you want to sit and listen, offer a few thoughts, or even express a surface level of your own pain, go ahead. But don't neglect what brings you to this place—that longing for meaning. You can't ignore it away. Dip your feet in the water of brutally honest discussion, and you may choose to dive in. There is healing here.

Stay on task. Refrain from sharing material that falls into the "too much information" category. Don't spill unnecessary stuff, such as your wife's penchant for midnight bedroom belly dancing or your boss's obsession with Jennifer Aniston. This is about discovering how you can be a better person.

   If structure isn't your group's strength, try a few minutes of general comments about the study, and then take each "Live" question one at a time and give everyone in the group a chance to respond. That should get you into the meat of matters pretty quickly.

Hold each other accountable. That "Live" section is an important gear in the growth machine. If you're really ready for positive change—for spiritual growth—you'll want to take this section seriously. Not only should you personally be thorough as you summarize your discoveries, practical as you compose your goals, and realistic as you determine the plan for accountability, you must hold everyone else in the group accountable for doing these things. Be lovingly, brutally honest as you examine each other's "Live" section. Don't hold back—this is where the rubber meets the road. A lack of openness here may send other group members skidding off that road.

MY JOB

> "I'm stuck in a dead-end job,
> not living the dream I once had."

THE BEGINNING PLACE

We start each lesson by asking you to do a sometimes-difficult thing: determine the core truths about the study topic as it relates to you today. Think about your job for a moment. Wait—don't lose that first thought. Did you scowl? Groan? Let out an audible, exhausted sigh? Or did you smile?

The plans we make for our future don't always (usually?) look like the future we end up with. The career you were certain would be the perfect fit feels like a too-small, three-armed sweater within a week. The job you took so you could pay the bills is taking more from your spirit than it is paying you in dollars. And that promotion you'd been promised? It went instead to the cute blonde your boss has been ogling.

Are you where you thought you'd be when you first dreamed your career future? Which list is longer, your likes or your dislikes about your job? Dig around until you have a good starting place for this lesson. Be honest about the good, the bad, and the ugly. And here's a rule you can apply to every lesson in this series: Drop the word "fine" from your vocabulary. It's far too easy to use this word in place of what's really going on. "It's fine." "I'm fine, really." Are you? If you hate your job, say so. If you're bored, lost, unhappy, disappointed—or thrilled, challenged, hopeful—say that, too.

Use the space below to summarize your beginning place for this lesson. Describe your workplace reality as well as your dreams. We'll start here and then go deeper.

AFTER MY RETIREMENT FROM THE ARMY IN 1970, I SPENT THE FIRST 3 MONTHS FIXING UP THE HOUSE I'D OWNED FOR 15 YEARS BUT HAD NEVER LIVED IN UNTIL THEN.

ONE MORNING — CUT GRASS. NO - DID THAT YESTERDAY. CAN'T STAND IT - GOT TO DO SOMETHING. A JOB?

WENT BACK TO SCHOOL AND WORKED PART TIME. ANOTHER CAREER? MAYBE BUT WHAT?

READ For the Sake of a Two-Week Vacation

From *Death of a Salesman*, by Arthur Miller [1]

BIFF: "I tell ya, Hap, I don't know what the future is. I don't know—what I'm supposed to want."

HAPPY: "What do you mean?"

BIFF: "Well, I spent six or seven years after high school trying to work myself up. Shipping clerk, salesman, business of one kind or another. And it's a measly manner of existence. To get on that subway on the hot mornings in summer. To devote your whole life to keeping stock, or making phone calls, or selling or buying. To suffer fifty weeks of the year for the sake of a two-week vacation, when all you really desire is to be outdoors, with your shirt off."

THINK

- In what ways are you just working "for the sake of a two-week vacation"?
- How does the reality of your job situation today compare with the plans or dreams you had when you first entered the workforce?
- What's the driving motivation for your work? How has that changed over the years?

PRAY

Lord, help me to see . . .

READ You Think *Your* Job Is Tough . . .

Exodus 5:1–6:8

After that Moses and Aaron approached Pharaoh. They said, "GOD, the God of Israel, says, 'Free my people so that they can hold a festival for me in the wilderness.'"

Pharaoh said, "And who is GOD that I should listen to him and send Israel off? I know nothing of this so-called 'GOD' and I'm certainly not going to send Israel off."

They said, "The God of the Hebrews has met with us. Let us take a three-day journey into the wilderness so we can worship our GOD lest he strike us with either disease or death."

But the king of Egypt said, "Why on earth, Moses and Aaron, would you suggest the people be given a holiday? Back to work!" Pharaoh went on, "Look, I've got all these people bumming around, and now you want to reward them with time off?"

Pharaoh took immediate action. He sent down orders to the slave-drivers and their underlings: "Don't provide straw for the people for making bricks as you have been doing. Make them get their own straw. And make them produce the same number of bricks—no reduction in their daily quotas! They're getting lazy. They're going around saying, 'Give us time off so we can worship our God.' Crack down on them. That'll cure them of their whining, their god-fantasies."

The slave-drivers and their underlings went out to the people with their new instructions. "Pharaoh's orders: No more straw provided. Get your own straw wherever you can find it. And not one brick less in your daily work quota!" The people scattered all over Egypt scrabbling for straw.

The slave-drivers were merciless, saying, "Complete your daily quota of bricks—the same number as when you were given straw."

The Israelite foremen whom the slave-drivers had appointed were beaten and badgered. "Why didn't you finish your quota of bricks yesterday or the day before—and now again today!"

The Israelite foremen came to Pharaoh and cried out for

relief: "Why are you treating your servants like this? Nobody gives us any straw and they tell us, 'Make bricks!' Look at us—we're being beaten. And it's not our fault."

But Pharaoh said, "Lazy! That's what you are! Lazy! That's why you whine, 'Let us go so we can worship GOD.' Well then, go—go back to work. Nobody's going to give you straw, and at the end of the day you better bring in your full quota of bricks."

The Israelite foremen saw that they were in a bad way, having to go back and tell their workers, "Not one brick short in your daily quota."

As they left Pharaoh, they found Moses and Aaron waiting to meet them. The foremen said to them, "May GOD see what you've done and judge you—you've made us stink before Pharaoh and his servants! You've put a weapon in his hand that's going to kill us!"

Moses went back to GOD and said, "My Master, why are you treating this people so badly? And why did you ever send me? From the moment I came to Pharaoh to speak in your name, things have only gotten worse for this people. And rescue? Does this look like rescue to you?"

GOD said to Moses, "Now you'll see what I'll do to Pharaoh: With a strong hand he'll send them out free; with a strong hand he'll drive them out of his land."

God continued speaking to Moses, reassuring him, "I am GOD. I appeared to Abraham, Isaac, and Jacob as The Strong God, but by my name GOD (I-Am-Present) I was not known to them. I also established my covenant with them to give them the land of Canaan, the country in which they lived as sojourners. But now I've heard the groanings of the Israelites whom the Egyptians continue to enslave and I've remembered my covenant. Therefore tell the Israelites:

"I am GOD. I will bring you out from under the cruel hard labor of Egypt. I will rescue you from slavery. I will redeem you, intervening with great acts of judgment. I'll take you as my own people and I'll be God to you. You'll know that I am GOD, *your*

God who brings you out from under the cruel hard labor of Egypt. I'll bring you into the land that I promised to give Abraham, Isaac, and Jacob and give it to you as your own country. *I AM GOD.*"

THINK

- When in your work life have you felt like the Israelites in this story?
- How do you respond when you're overwhelmed with work or when work seems unfair?
- If you feel oppressed by your work, what would "deliverance" look like to you?
- What might be packaged in the "groanings" you express to God about work? What is it that you long for in the workplace?
- What might God's purpose be for the difficulties you're encountering at work today?

PRAY

God, lead me to . . .

READ The Imperfect Workplace

From the *Fast Company* article "Lesson One: Job Stuff"[2]

Is the workplace a forum for community? Do we find friendship, comfort, and a sense of belonging in the company canteen? Some social critics decry the erosion of civic communities, as evidenced by declining rates of volunteerism and bowling-league membership. In the new economy, they argue, everyone is working so much that a different sort of community has emerged within the confines of the corporate office park.

But that's not how our survey respondents see it. For most of them, the notion of finding community at work is another new-economy myth. If anything, many people appear to be disengaging themselves from the social aspects of their work, seeking a balanced life in which personal fulfillment doesn't depend so completely on their job.

We asked respondents to characterize their relationships with colleagues at work. More than one-third (36%) say that they would be friends with their coworkers "even if we didn't work together." Those who develop such bonds tend to be younger. Among people in their forties and fifties, just 30% view their colleagues as friends. In any case, slightly more than half of all respondents (50.3%) agree with the statement "My coworkers and I make a good team, but we're not friends." And 9% say that while they tolerate their officemates, they "would rather not work with them."

Regardless of how we feel about our colleagues, we spend a lot of time at work. On average, respondents reported working 41 hours "at an office or somewhere else outside the home" and working 6.5 hours at home. And they spend about 9 hours thinking about their job while doing "nonwork activities."

But at day's end, most people are able to leave work behind. We proposed a scenario: "You've had a bad day at work. One project bombed, and another project received a mediocre reception from a customer. The boss grumbled. A coworker quit." In the face of such a disastrous day, 46% of respondents said they would be "relieved just to be away from the office," while 29% claimed that they would be "able to leave work behind and to enjoy [their] home life." Only about one-quarter predicted that they would come home "in a horrible mood because of the day's events."

We concede, first of all, that the workplace is as imperfect as the people who populate it. The new-economy canon sounds great—but amid the thicket of human aspirations, emotions, and politics, it doesn't always work out as advertised. The workplace isn't a perfect substitute for community. The ideal of being paid according to one's value still gives way to more conventional (and less democratic) reward systems. And people don't always get the autonomy or the respect that they deserve. What can we say? The new economy didn't promise you a rose garden: It only promised a better system than the one created by the old economy.

We also suggest that expectations are often meant to be broken. We asked respondents to compare the work that they dreamed of pursuing when they left college with the job that they have today. Remarkably, given the impossibly lofty ideals and ambitions that are typical of people fresh out of college, only 44% of respondents admit that their work today isn't as fulfilling as they had expected it to be. Yet, even among those who like or love their jobs, 38% say that their current work doesn't match what they had once hoped for.

THINK

- Have you experienced the perfect workplace? What does it look like?
- How important is it for you to find community in the workplace? How are you finding it in your present situation?
- How much of your work (whether actual work or simply work attitudes) comes home with you each day? Is that something you want to change? If so, how?
- In what ways has your job not worked out "as advertised"?

- How fulfilling is your work today? How does that compare with what you'd hoped for?

PRAY

Father, give me patience to . . .

READ Getting By

Ecclesiastes 2:17-26

I hate life. As far as I can see, what happens on earth is a bad business. It's smoke—and spitting into the wind.

And I hated everything I'd accomplished and accumulated on this earth. I can't take it with me—no, I have to leave it to whoever comes after me. Whether they're worthy or worthless—and who's to tell?—they'll take over the earthly results of my intense thinking and hard work. Smoke.

That's when I called it quits, gave up on anything that could be hoped for on this earth. What's the point of working your fingers to the bone if you hand over what you worked for to someone who never lifted a finger for it? Smoke, that's what it is. A bad business from start to finish. So what do you get from a life of hard labor? Pain and grief from dawn to dusk. Never a decent night's rest. Nothing but smoke.

The best you can do with your life is have a good time and get by the best you can. The way I see it, that's it—divine fate. Whether we feast or fast, it's up to God. God may give wisdom and knowledge and joy to his favorites, but sinners are assigned a life of hard labor, and end up turning their wages over to God's favorites. Nothing but smoke—and spitting into the wind.

THINK

- What's your first response to the passage above?
- In what ways do you feel like your work life is nothing more than spitting into the wind?
- What does this passage really say about your "life of hard labor"?
- How do you "get by the best you can" at work?
- What is God's role in both the "feasting" and the "fasting" seasons in your work life? Does that really add comfort, meaning, or purpose to your work? Explain.

THINK (CONTINUED)

PRAY

God, show me your role in . . .

READ Finding Meaning

From the *Fortune* article "Why Do We Work?" by Brian Dumaine[3]

In the days of misty towers, distressed maidens, and stalwart knights, a young man, walking down a road, came upon a laborer fiercely pounding away at a stone with hammer and chisel. The lad asked the worker, who looked frustrated and angry, "What are you doing?" The laborer answered in a pained voice: "I'm trying to shape this stone, and it is backbreaking work." The youth continued his journey and soon came upon another man chipping away at a similar stone, who looked neither particularly angry nor happy. "What are you doing?" he asked. "I'm shaping a stone for a building." The young man went on and before long came to a third worker chipping away at a stone, but this worker was singing happily as he worked. "What are you doing?" The worker smiled and replied: "I'm building a cathedral."

When you ask people why they work, most will tell you, in a tone usually reserved for slow children and dimwitted in-laws, that they do it for the money. But if that's entirely true, how do you explain people like Warren Buffett or Bill Gates, whose combined net worth is greater than the GDP of Luxembourg and yet who throw themselves into their jobs as if their next meal depended on it? Or why do so many lottery winners, after a few months of champagne, oysters, and a suite at the Ritz, end up punching a clock again, if not at their old job, at some other kind of work? When Robert Weiss, a research professor at the University of Massachusetts, asked people in a survey whether they'd work if they had inherited enough to live comfortably, roughly eight out of ten people said yes.

So if it's not only money, what is it? More and more people today—and the trend is particularly advanced among baby boomers—are looking to work to satisfy some deeply individualistic, emotional, and psychological need. Now that the boomers have hit middle age and become morbidly preoccupied with their mortality, this most self-indulgent of all generations is beginning to ask hard questions about work and what it all means. . . .

If the old sources of meaning don't hold any longer, where are people turning? Like the medieval stonecutter who chose to find his own meaning for his work, people are looking within themselves rather than to the corporation. As John Geraci, the COO of Blessing-White, a New Jersey consulting firm, puts it, "Today the new creed is, 'I am what I do, not where I work.'" What form does this new, personalized search for meaning take? When *Fortune* asked scores of managers, from CEOs to warehouse supervisors, why they worked, the three most common reasons cited besides paying the mortgage were to make the world a better place, to help themselves and others on their team grow spiritually and intellectually, and lastly, to perfect their technical skills.

THINK

- Which stonecutter best represents your approach to work?
- If you had enough money to never "punch a clock" again, would you stop working? Why or why not?
- What needs do you try to satisfy through your work?
- How do you find meaning in your work? What is the spiritual dimension to your work?

PRAY

Lord, teach me to find meaning . . .

READ Yeah, Right.

Ephesians 6:5-9

Servants, respectfully obey your earthly masters but always with an eye to obeying the *real* master, Christ. Don't just do what you have to do to get by, but work heartily, as Christ's servants doing what God wants you to do. And work with a smile on your face, always keeping in mind that no matter who happens to be giving the orders, you're really serving God. Good work will get you good pay from the Master, regardless of whether you are slave or free.

Masters, it's the same with you. No abuse, please, and no threats. You and your servants are both under the same Master in heaven. He makes no distinction between you and them.

Colossians 3:22-25

Servants, do what you're told by your earthly masters. And don't just do the minimum that will get you by. Do your best. Work from the heart for your real Master, for God, confident that you'll get paid in full when you come into your inheritance. Keep in mind always that the ultimate Master you're serving is Christ. The sullen servant who does shoddy work will be held responsible. Being Christian doesn't cover up bad work.

THINK

- What does God want from you in the workplace?
- How would you summarize the message of these passages in real-world terms in the context of your workplace?
- What obstacles do you face in fulfilling the challenge of these passages?
- You may love, despise, or simply feel neutral toward your earthly boss, but he or she is not God. How do you reconcile the realities of the workplace with this spiritual challenge to work from the heart as if for God?

THINK (CONTINUED)

PRAY

God, give me wisdom to . . .

READ Best Thing You Can Do?

Romans 12:1-2

So here's what I want you to do, God helping you: Take your everyday, ordinary life—your sleeping, eating, going-to-work, and walking-around life—and place it before God as an offering. Embracing what God does for you is the best thing you can do for him. Don't become so well-adjusted to your culture that you fit into it without even thinking. Instead, fix your attention on God. You'll be changed from the inside out. Readily recognize what he wants from you, and quickly respond to it. Unlike the culture around you, always dragging you down to its level of immaturity, God brings the best out of you, develops well-formed maturity in you.

From the *Health Services Network* article "Finding Meaning, Happiness in Your Work," by Sondra Farrell Bazrod[4]

Seeing your job as a way to help someone is a key way of finding satisfaction, said Sidney Walter, a former UCLA psychology professor who now works as a forensic psychologist for the U.S. Department of Health and Human Services. "Unfortunately, many people don't realize this," said Walter. "I've asked thousands of people, 'What's the purpose of your job?' and most will answer, 'To make money.' This is true of all types of workers, from lawyers to janitors."

Walter recommends people discover and accept the purpose of their jobs.

"It is not for you to earn money," he said. "It is to serve others. All occupations have the same purpose—helping others. The teacher to educate, the baseball player to entertain, the shoe clerk to assist, the jailer, vendor, seamstress and spouse to help, assist, to aid others. Until this is recognized and accepted, you cannot be happy at your job."

THINK

- In what ways have you become so "well-adjusted to your [work] culture" that you don't even think about it?
- How is it possible to take your "going-to-work life" and give it to God as an offering? What does that look like?
- How does fixing your attention on God give you hope in the workplace?
- If you feel your work culture is dragging you down, what are your options? How should you respond?
- How does the way you view your job affect the way you relate to the work culture?
- How does the work you do help others? How does that perspective impact the way you do your job? The way you interact with others at work?

PRAY

Lord, thank you for . . .

LIVE

What I Want to Discuss

What have you discovered this week that you definitely want to discuss with your small group? Write that here. Then begin your small-group discussion with these thoughts.

So What?

Use the following space to summarize the truths you uncovered about your job, your attitude toward your job, and what you really need to do to move out of a "treading water" mindset. Review your "Beginning Place" if you need to remember where you began. How does God's truth impact the "next step" in your journey?

Then What?

What is one practical thing you can do to apply what you've discovered? Describe how you would put this into practice. What steps would you take? Remember to think realistically—an admirable but unreachable goal is as good as no goal. Discuss your goal in your small group to further define it.

How?

Identify how you will be held accountable to the goal you described. Who will be on your support team? What are their responsibilities? How will you measure the success of your plan? Write the details here.

MY ACCOMPLISHMENTS

"I haven't achieved what I dreamed I might."

A REMINDER:

Before you dive into this study, spend a little time reviewing what you wrote in the previous lesson's "Live" sections. How are you doing? Check with your small-group members and review your progress toward the specified goals. If necessary, adjust your goals and plans, and then recommit to them.

THE BEGINNING PLACE

For many men, one of their saddest moments comes the day they realize (or finally acknowledge) that the big baseball, basketball, or football star they watch on TV is significantly younger than they are (and making millions of dollars playing a game). Or perhaps it's the day they meet the new boss only to discover he or she is barely old enough to vote. In these moments, we momentarily forget all the good we've done and focus instead on our failures. Most of us didn't become the famous businessmen, actors, sports heroes, or rock stars we once thought we'd be.

That realization sends men down one of two paths. Some discover a renewed vigor to accomplish "something." Anything. Others settle into reluctant acceptance that "it wasn't meant to be" and give up on dreams. All those plans that looked promising years ago suddenly morph into memories of what could have been. Doubt, disappointment, and sometimes despair creep into the now, threatening to hobble the drive that birthed those dreams in the first place.

So where are you now? What is the first thing that comes to mind when you think about your accomplishments? What have you checked off your life to-do list? Do you still have the same motivation to accomplish big things that you did last year? Five years ago? And what about that word "success"? What did it once mean to you? Does it mean the same thing today?

Use the space below to summarize your beginning place for this lesson. Describe your reality as well as your dreams. We'll start here and then go deeper.

READ Bootstraps

Job 6:8-13

All I want is an answer to one prayer,
a last request to be honored:
Let God step on me—squash me like a bug,
and be done with me for good.
I'd at least have the satisfaction
of not having blasphemed the Holy God,
before being pressed past the limits.
Where's the strength to keep my hopes up?
What future do I have to keep me going?
Do you think I have nerves of steel?
Do you think I'm made of iron?
Do you think I can pull myself up by my bootstraps?
Why, I don't even have any boots!

THINK

- When have you felt like Job—wishing God would just step on you and put you out of your misery?
- What obstacles keep you from accomplishing important goals?
- When have you been pressed to perform to your limits? What was the result?

PRAY

God, help me to see . . .

READ Great Big Goals

From "Special Message to the Congress on Urgent National Needs," by President John F. Kennedy[1]

I believe that this nation should commit itself to achieving the goal, before this decade is out, of landing a man on the moon and returning him safely to the earth. No single space project in this period will be more impressive to mankind, or more important for the long-range exploration of space; and none will be so difficult or expensive to accomplish. We propose to accelerate the development of the appropriate lunar space craft. We propose to develop alternate liquid and solid fuel boosters, much larger than any now being developed, until certain which is superior. We propose additional funds for other engine development and for unmanned explorations—explorations which are particularly important for one purpose which this nation will never overlook: the survival of the man who first makes this daring flight. But in a very real sense, it will not be one man going to the moon—if we make this judgment affirmatively, it will be an entire nation. For all of us must work to put him there.

Let it be clear—and this is a judgment which the Members of the Congress must finally make—let it be clear that I am asking the Congress and the country to accept a firm commitment to a new course of action, a course which will last for many years and carry very heavy costs: 531 million dollars in fiscal '62—an estimated seven to nine billion dollars additional over the next five years. If we are to go only half way, or reduce our sights in the face of difficulty, in my judgment it would be better not to go at all.

Amos 5:21-24

"I can't stand your religious meetings.
I'm fed up with your conferences and conventions.
I want nothing to do with your religion projects,
your pretentious slogans and goals.

I'm sick of your fund-raising schemes,
  your public relations and image making.
I've had all I can take of your noisy ego-music.
  When was the last time you sang to *me*?
Do you know what I want?
  I want justice—oceans of it.
I want fairness—rivers of it.
  That's what I want. That's *all* I want."

THINK

- In his speech, President Kennedy boldly stated, "If we are to go only half way . . . it would be better not to go at all." What are the benefits of this kind of thinking? The risks? The dangers?
- How many of your goals are prompted by competition or one-upmanship? What drives such an approach?
- In the Amos passage, God seems to be speaking to people who had big goals. What does this tell you about what's important to God?
- Do you run your goals and dreams through a "what does God want" filter? How would/does that modify your goals and dreams?

PRAY

Father, give me the confidence to . . .

READ   In the Midst of Failure

Jeremiah 45:2-5

These are the words of GOD, the God of Israel, to you, Baruch. You say, "These are bad times for me! It's one thing after another. GOD is piling on the pain. I'm worn out and there's no end in sight."

But GOD says, "Look around. What I've built I'm about to wreck, and what I've planted I'm about to rip up. And I'm doing it everywhere—all over the whole earth! So forget about making any big plans for yourself. Things are going to get worse before they get better. But don't worry. I'll keep you alive through the whole business."

THINK

- When have you felt that God was messing up your plans by "piling on the pain"? How did you respond?
- How do you deal with situations that look like they're going to "get worse before they get better"?
- Is knowing God will "keep you alive through the whole business" enough for you to deal with shattered dreams and broken plans? What is your greatest challenge in circumstances like this?

PRAY

Lord, comfort me when . . .

READ No Motivation

From *Dangers Men Face*, by Jerry White[2]

One thing is sure. At some point, every man will suffer moderate to severe loss of motivation. When it happens we become confused. We recognize it but feel powerless to change our feelings.

It is frightening, especially for men who are used to being motivated and excited about life. There comes a sense of purposelessness, a lack of drive, a feeling that nothing matters. An inability to act takes over. Critical tasks remain undone. Going to work is drudgery. And all of this spills over into family life, causing conflicts and misunderstandings. . . .

Many paths lead to a loss of motivation. Personality is a factor. So is age and stage of life. Life traumas contribute. Failing health exacerbates the problem. Sometimes we call it burnout.

We despise the feelings and silently cry to be rescued.

But that is the problem. The cry is usually silent. Men find it so difficult to call for help. We go on and suffer in silence rather than admit the weakness we have seen in ourselves.

THINK

- When have you experienced a loss of motivation? What prompted it?
- How might unreached goals or missed accomplishments impact your motivation?
- What is your typical response to a personal loss of motivation?
- When you feel burned out, do you "suffer in silence," or "call for help"?
- What are the risks of staying silent about burnout?
- What level of "motivation loss" do you feel today? Do you see an end to it? How will you get there?

THINK (CONTINUED)

PRAY

God, motivate me to . . .

READ Interrupted Plans

Romans 1:8-17

I thank God through Jesus for every one of you. That's first. People everywhere keep telling me about your lives of faith, and every time I hear them, I thank him. And God, whom I so love to worship and serve by spreading the good news of his Son— the Message!—knows that every time I think of you in my prayers, which is practically all the time, I ask him to clear the way for me to come and see you. The longer this waiting goes on, the deeper the ache. I so want to be there to deliver God's gift in person and watch you grow stronger right before my eyes! But don't think I'm not expecting to get something out of this, too! You have as much to give me as I do to you.

Please don't misinterpret my failure to visit you, friends. You have no idea how many times I've made plans for Rome. I've been determined to get some personal enjoyment out of God's work among you, as I have in so many other non-Jewish towns and communities. But something has always come up and pre-vented it. Everyone I meet—it matters little whether they're man-nered or rude, smart or simple—deepens my sense of interde-pendence and obligation. And that's why I can't wait to get to you in Rome, preaching this wonderful good news of God.

It's news I'm most proud to proclaim, this extraordinary Message of God's powerful plan to rescue everyone who trusts him, starting with Jews and then right on to everyone else! God's way of putting people right shows up in the acts of faith, con-firming what Scripture has said all along: "The person in right standing before God by trusting him really lives."

THINK

- In this passage, Paul described his failure to accomplish an important visit. In what ways does that remind you of your life—your intent to meet with friends or reach other goals?

- Paul asked his letter readers not to misinterpret his failure to visit. How have you dealt with others (family, friends, worker associates) who are impacted by your unfulfilled or interrupted plans?
- Where does the phrase "Something came up" appear in your life? Is that phrase ever an excuse rather than the truth?
- What happens to long-term goals when short-term plans keep going unfulfilled?
- What was Paul's implicit advice about following through on plans?

PRAY

Lord, help me to follow through . . .

READ The Money Factor

From the *Fast Company* article "Money and the Meaning of Life," by
Michael S. Malone[3]

Having lots of money can be like a drug. It can make you feel
powerful and giddy. It can convince you that everything's going
to be okay. Years ago they asked the great fighter Joe Louis what
he thought about money, and he said, "I don't like money very
much, but it calms my nerves." Money makes us unjustifiably feel
that we're better and more important than we really are. When
money can make you feel humble, then I think it's really useful.
But if it fattens your ego, which it often does, then look out.

That way lies madness. That's what all the Greek tragedies
are about—hubris—and that's part of the problem with money.
It is greatness, it is power, it is beauty. Money is about love and
relationships. It has a wonderful power to bring people together
as well as tear them apart. You can't escape money. If you run
from it, it will chase you and catch you. Even Thoreau today
would need a real estate agent to help him buy the cabin at
Walden Pond.

If we don't understand our relationship to money in this culture, then I think we're doomed. If you don't know how you are
toward money and really understand that relationship, you simply don't know yourself. Period. . . .

As the ancients said, we are angels and devils at the same
time—and sometimes it's hard to distinguish between the two.
Sometimes the two masquerade as each other. Caring for your
friends and family and children is part of being in this world,
though it may seem a spiritual act. Getting your kid through college
is not a spiritual act but part of being in the world. At the same
time, working and making money can have a spiritual dimension.

We philosophers can't really figure this out better than anyone else. And money alone can't buy you an answer. Only
worldly experience with lots of adventures and making lots of
money may finally let you come away from it saying, "There's

something money can't buy. I can't put my finger on it, but I sense it." . . .

You should be looking for the joy, the struggle, and the challenge of work. What you bring forth from your own guts and heart. The happiness of hard work. No amount of money can buy that. Those are things of the spirit.

1 Timothy 6:3-10

If you have leaders there who teach otherwise, who refuse the solid words of our Master Jesus and this godly instruction, tag them for what they are: ignorant windbags who infect the air with germs of envy, controversy, bad-mouthing, suspicious rumors. Eventually there's an epidemic of backstabbing, and truth is but a distant memory. They think religion is a way to make a fast buck.

A devout life does bring wealth, but it's the rich simplicity of being yourself before God. Since we entered the world penniless and will leave it penniless, if we have bread on the table and shoes on our feet, that's enough.

But if it's only money these leaders are after, they'll self-destruct in no time. Lust for money brings trouble and nothing but trouble. Going down that path, some lose their footing in the faith completely and live to regret it bitterly ever after.

From *The Treasure Principle*, by Randy Alcorn[4]

Recently I was attending a gathering of givers. We went around the room and told our stories. The words *fun, joy, exciting,* and *wonderful* kept resurfacing. There were lots of smiles and laughter, along with tears of joy. One older couple eagerly shared how they are always traveling around the world, getting involved in the ministries they're giving to. Meanwhile, their home in the States is becoming run-down. They said, "Our children keep telling us, 'Fix up your house or buy a new one. You can afford it.' We tell them, 'Why would we do that? That's not what excites us!'"

THINK

- How does money make you feel better than you really are? How can it make you feel worse? Do you agree that money is like a drug? Explain.
- What percentage of your goals and dreams are essentially about money or "stuff"?
- The spiritual "wealth" of a devout life sounds great, but it doesn't pay the bills. How do you reconcile the real-world demands for making money with the spiritual warning about the lust for money?
- Wrestle with your desire to be a success in terms of monetary wealth and the message of 1 Timothy. What makes this a sticky issue for you?
- How do you feel when you give money away? What does that do to your faith?

PRAY

God, teach me your truth about . . .

READ Where True Accomplishments Begin

Job 12:13-16

> True wisdom and real power belong to God;
>> from him we learn how to live,
>> and also what to live for.
> If he tears something down, it's down for good;
>> if he locks people up, they're locked up for good.
> If he holds back the rain, there's a drought;
>> if he lets it loose, there's a flood.
> Strength and success belong to God;
>> both deceived and deceiver must answer to him.

THINK

- What does this passage say about accomplishments?
- What role does God play in success?
- Practically speaking, what does it look like to "learn how to live, and also what to live for" from God?
- How does that play out in your everyday life?
- If "strength and success" belong to God, how does that affect the way you look at your accomplishments and failures?

PRAY

Father, you know that I . . .

LIVE

What I Want to Discuss

What have you discovered this week that you definitely want to discuss with your small group? Write that here. Then begin your small-group discussion with these thoughts.

So What?

Use the following space to summarize the truths you uncovered about your accomplishments and what you really need to do to move out of a "treading water" mindset. Review your "Beginning Place" if you need to remember where you began. How does God's truth impact the "next step" in your journey?

Then What?

What is one practical thing you can do to apply what you've discovered? Describe how you would put this into practice. What steps would you take? Remember to think realistically—an admirable but unreachable goal is as good as no goal. Discuss your goal in your small group to further define it.

How?

Identify how you will be held accountable to the goal you described. Who will be on your support team? What are their responsibilities? How will you measure the success of your plan? Write the details here.

MY
FRIENDS

"My friends disappoint me, and I, them."

A REMINDER:

Before you dive into this study, spend a little time reviewing what you wrote in the previous lesson's "Live" sections. How are you doing? Check with your small-group members and review your progress toward the specified goals. If necessary, adjust your goals and plans, and then recommit to them.

THE BEGINNING PLACE

Friends illustrate the best and worst in life. They slap congratulations on your back one minute and stab you in the back the next, challenge you to do the right thing today and challenge your ability to do the right thing tomorrow. You may know a little something about this (after all, you're a friend, too). But there is something about friendship that demands our attention.

Take a moment to think about the status of your friendships. (If you're married, we'll exclude that particular relationship at the moment. Same goes for a budding romantic relationship if you're not married.) Who are the people you call "friend" and mean it? What defines that relationship? Do you have one or more friends you can count on—really count on? (These are the people who love you unconditionally and are just as likely to encourage you as to call you to task for questionable choices.) What about casual relationships—what do those friendships look like?

Now consider each of these friendships from a different perspective: What are the greatest disappointments you experience with these friends? Do you ever feel you just don't have the energy to be a good friend, to intentionally seek out a friend? Why? What causes that?

Use the space below to summarize your beginning place for this lesson. Describe your friendship reality as well as your dreams. We'll start here and then go deeper.

READ The Failed Friendship

From the ChristianityToday.com article "Why Friends Fail," by Les and Leslie Parrott[1]

There is a line in Woody Allen's film *Annie Hall* where he says to Diane Keaton, "A relationship, I think, is like a shark, you know? It has to constantly move forward or it dies. And I think what we got on our hands is a dead shark." Some friendships die because they aren't moving forward; they die from stagnation or plain old neglect. You meant to call but didn't. You knew it was his birthday but were too busy to celebrate (you knew he'd understand). But friendships need to be nurtured. It's as simple as that. Without nurturance, annoyance is sure to set in. Think about it. When we're busy we only do what comes easy, and even good friendships aren't always easy. So if your friend has an annoying trait, if [he's] loud, or cheap, or a habitual complainer, for example, you are more likely to neglect the relationship. Of course the same is true in the opposite direction when your friend is neglecting you. Whether it's you or [him], however, neglect is sure to cause a rift. And when it does, it almost always catches us off guard, surprising us when we least expect it and can least handle it: when we're going through stressful times at school, work, or home that make us less attentive, and less able to respond—which is what caused the neglect to begin with. That's why it can seem that the best friendships fail precisely when we need them the most.

THINK

- Think about the friendships you have now and those you once had. In what ways are those friendships like "sharks" needing to move forward?
- What are your most significant obstacles to maintaining friendships?
- In what ways do you do "what comes easy" in relationships?

- How have you felt neglected in a friendship? How have you neglected others?
- What are some practical ways to stay connected with good friends, so they're "in the loop" when you need them most?

PRAY

Lord, help me stay close to . . .

READ What Good Are Bad Friends?

Job 6:14-30

When desperate people give up on God Almighty,
    their friends, at least, should stick with them.
But my brothers are fickle as a gulch in the desert—
    one day they're gushing with water
From melting ice and snow
    cascading out of the mountains,
But by midsummer they're dry,
    gullies baked dry in the sun.
Travelers who spot them and go out of their way for a drink,
    end up in a waterless gulch and die of thirst.
Merchant caravans from Tema see them and expect water,
    tourists from Sheba hope for a cool drink.
They arrive so confident—but what a disappointment!
    They get there, and their faces fall!
And you, my so-called friends, are no better—there's
      nothing to you!
    One look at a hard scene and you shrink in fear.
It's not as though I asked you for anything—
    I didn't ask you for one red cent—
Nor did I beg you to go out on a limb for me.
    So why all this dodging and shuffling?

Confront me with the truth and I'll shut up,
    show me where I've gone off the track.
Honest words never hurt anyone,
    but what's the point of all this pious bluster?
You pretend to tell me what's wrong with my life,
    but treat my words of anguish as so much hot air.
Are people mere things to you?
    Are friends just items of profit and loss?

Look me in the eyes!
    Do you think I'd lie to your face?
Think it over—no double-talk!
    Think carefully—my integrity is on the line!
Can you detect anything false in what I say?
    Don't you trust me to discern good from evil?

THINK

- What experience do you have with friends who offer questionable advice?
- How have you been a "so-called friend" to others?
- How can honest words help a relationship? In what circumstances might they damage a friendship?
- React to Job's question "Are friends just items of profit and loss?"
- What do you want from a friend: brutal honesty or polite (and sometimes unmerited) support? What do you usually give and receive?

PRAY

God, shape my language by . . .

READ Embarrassingly Good Friends

1 Samuel 20:1-42

David got out of Naioth in Ramah alive and went to Jonathan. "What do I do now? What wrong have I inflicted on your father that makes him so determined to kill me?"

"Nothing," said Jonathan. "You've done nothing wrong. And you're not going to die. Really, you're not! My father tells me everything. He does nothing, whether big or little, without confiding in me. So why would he do this behind my back? It can't be."

But David said, "Your father knows that we are the best of friends. So he says to himself, 'Jonathan must know nothing of this. If he does, he'll side with David.' But it's true—as sure as GOD lives, and as sure as you're alive before me right now—he's determined to kill me."

Jonathan said, "Tell me what you have in mind. I'll do anything for you."

David said, "Tomorrow marks the New Moon. I'm scheduled to eat dinner with the king. Instead, I'll go hide in the field until the evening of the third. If your father misses me, say, 'David asked if he could run down to Bethlehem, his hometown, for an anniversary reunion, and worship with his family.' If he says, 'Good!' then I'm safe. But if he gets angry, you'll know for sure that he's made up his mind to kill me. Oh, stick with me in this. You've entered into a covenant of GOD with me, remember! If I'm in the wrong, go ahead and kill me yourself. Why bother giving me up to your father?"

"Never!" exclaimed Jonathan. "I'd never do that! If I get the slightest hint that my father is fixated on killing you, I'll tell you."

David asked, "And whom will you get to tell me if your father comes back with a harsh answer?"

"Come outside," said Jonathan. "Let's go to the field." When the two of them were out in the field, Jonathan said, "As GOD, the God of Israel, is my witness, by this time tomorrow I'll get it out of my father how he feels about you. Then I'll let you know what I learn. May GOD do his worst to me if I let you down! If my father still intends to kill you, I'll tell you and get you out of here in one piece. And GOD be with you as he's been with my father! If I make it through this alive, continue to be my covenant friend. And if I die, keep the covenant friendship with my family—forever. And when GOD finally rids the earth of David's enemies, stay loyal to Jonathan!" Jonathan repeated his pledge of love and friendship for David. He loved David more than his own soul!

Jonathan then laid out his plan: "Tomorrow is the New Moon, and you'll be missed when you don't show up for dinner. On the third day, when they've quit expecting you, come to the place where you hid before, and wait beside that big boulder. I'll shoot three arrows in the direction of the boulder. Then I'll send off my servant, 'Go find the arrows.' If I yell after the servant, 'The arrows are on this side! Retrieve them!' that's the signal that you can return safely—as GOD lives, not a thing to fear! But if I yell, 'The arrows are farther out!' then run for it—GOD wants you out of here! Regarding all the things we've discussed, remember that GOD's in on this with us to the very end!"

David hid in the field. On the holiday of the New Moon, the king came to the table to eat. He sat where he always sat, the place against the wall, with Jonathan across the table and Abner at Saul's side. But David's seat was empty. Saul didn't mention it at the time, thinking, "Something's happened that's made him unclean. That's it—he's probably unclean for the holy meal."

But the day after the New Moon, day two of the holiday, David's seat was still empty. Saul asked Jonathan his son, "So where's that son of Jesse? He hasn't eaten with us either yesterday or today."

Jonathan said, "David asked my special permission to go to Bethlehem. He said, 'Give me leave to attend a family reunion back home. My brothers have ordered me to be there. If it seems all right to you, let me go and see my brothers.' That's why he's not here at the king's table."

Saul exploded in anger at Jonathan: "You son of a slut! Don't you think I know that you're in cahoots with the son of Jesse, disgracing both you and your mother? For as long as the son of Jesse is walking around free on this earth, your future in this kingdom is at risk. Now go get him. Bring him here. From this moment, he's as good as dead!"

Jonathan stood up to his father. "Why dead? What's he done?"

Saul threw his spear at him to kill him. That convinced Jonathan that his father was fixated on killing David.

Jonathan stormed from the table, furiously angry, and ate nothing the rest of the day, upset for David and smarting under the humiliation from his father.

In the morning, Jonathan went to the field for the appointment with David. He had his young servant with him. He told the servant, "Run and get the arrows I'm about to shoot." The boy started running and Jonathan shot an arrow way beyond him. As the boy came to the area where the arrow had been shot, Jonathan yelled out, "Isn't the arrow farther out?" He yelled again, "Hurry! Quickly! Don't just stand there!" Jonathan's servant then picked up the arrow and brought it to his master. The boy, of course, knew nothing of what was going on. Only Jonathan and David knew.

Jonathan gave his quiver and bow to the boy and sent him back to town. After the servant was gone, David got up from his hiding place beside the boulder, then fell on his face to the ground—three times prostrating himself! And then they kissed one another and wept, friend over friend, David weeping especially hard.

Jonathan said, "Go in peace! The two of us have vowed friendship in GOD's name, saying, 'GOD will be the bond between me and you, and between my children and your children forever!'"

THINK

- Do you have a friend like Jonathan? What does (or would) it mean to you to have a friend like that?
- The picture of David and Jonathan's friendship can seem like an unrealistic ideal. What aspects of this friendship do you have the hardest time applying in your own relationships?
- What are examples of a friend going "the extra mile" in a relationship with you? What lengths have you gone to in order to help a friend?
- What can you learn from David and Jonathan's friendship that can make yours stronger?
- What is your natural response to a friend willing to take risks to help and support you? What is the toughest thing about having a friend who is really "there" for you? The greatest benefit?

PRAY

God, thank you for . . .

READ Who Needs Friends?

From *The Four Loves*, by C. S. Lewis[2]

> Friendship is—in a sense not at all derogatory to it—the least
> natural of loves; the least instinctive, organic, biological, gregari-
> ous and necessary. It has least commerce with our nerves; there
> is nothing throaty about it; nothing that quickens the pulse or
> turns you red and pale. It is essentially between individuals; the
> moment two men are friends they have in some degree drawn
> apart together from the herd. Without Eros none of us would
> have been begotten and without Affection none of us would
> have been reared; but we can live and breed without Friendship.

Ecclesiastes 4:7-10

> I turned my head and saw yet another wisp of smoke on its way
> to nothingness: a solitary person, completely alone—no children,
> no family, no friends—yet working obsessively late into the
> night, compulsively greedy for more and more, never bothering
> to ask, "Why am I working like a dog, never having any fun? And
> who cares?" More smoke. A bad business.
>
> > It's better to have a partner than go it alone.
> > Share the work, share the wealth.
> > And if one falls down, the other helps,
> > But if there's no one to help, tough!

THINK

- What is your response to the claim that friendship is the "least
  instinctive, organic, biological, gregarious and necessary" of the
  loves?
- What is it that draws men "apart together from the herd"?
  What attributes in another make it worthwhile for you to seek
  friendship?

- If friendship isn't "necessary," what is its point? How does friendship make life better?
- In what ways have you isolated yourself from friendships? How do you relate to the writer of the Ecclesiastes passage?
- Think of a time when a friend has "shared the work." What did that look like? Why was that valuable to you?
- Would you ever prefer a quiet, solitary life to one filled with friends? Why or why not?

PRAY

Lord, help me to be . . .

READ The Value of Friends

From the *Wisconsin State Journal* article "Don't Underestimate the Value of Friends" [3]

It had been 24 years and 11 months since I last heard from Josh Crowell.

"This is the not-very reverend Joshua Crowell," the voice on my answering machine announced a week ago. "Betty Ann and I will be in Madison on July 10, and we wonder if you're free for lunch."

A quarter of a century ago, Josh Crowell and I were ecclesiastical buddies. He was the minister of the First Congregational Church in Evansville, and I was serving interim ministries in Madison-area churches as well as writing for the *Wisconsin State Journal.*

Josh baptized my kids. I goaded him into organizing the annual William R. Wineke Memorial Hymn Sing in Evansville. We were buddies. And, when Josh left Evansville to become minister of the First Congregational Church in Essex, Conn.—a post he still holds—I was devastated. We lost contact, though we didn't really lose touch. I periodically wrote him, calling him a jerk for not answering last year's letter. But I hadn't heard his voice for 24 years and 11 months until that telephone call.

So, we met Monday for lunch at Famous Dave's, a place known for carbohydrates and saturated fat. Within 10 seconds it was as if he'd never left. We spent virtually no time "catching up." We moved immediately into bizarre speculations on theology and the church and on our wayward colleagues. We were buddies once more.

Josh Crowell is one of the reasons I'm not in the least bit sorry about leaving middle-age behind and moving on to senior citizen status. There are things we learn that can be learned only through time and experience.

The most important is that a good friendship never disappears.

The things that bind friends together are intangible and, for the most part, indefinable. All I know is that when I am with

Josh Crowell I not only like being with him, but I like being with me as well.

I am a very fortunate guy because I get that same feeling from a fair number of people, some of whom I see weekly and others of whom I see only rarely.

Over the years we've all gotten older, fatter and, with a couple of exceptions, bald. Our children have grown up, gotten into trouble, settled down, gotten into more trouble and settled down again. Our careers blazed and sputtered and chugged along, creating for our families comfortable livings, though not the kind of fame and fortune we thought we would achieve. We've learned we aren't nearly as wise as we once thought we were and that our bodies aren't nearly as untiring as we hoped they were.

The one thing that's consistent, however, is that when we get together, whether we've been separated for a week, a year, or a quarter-century, we just start talking and laughing as if our conversation had been interrupted for only a few moments. Any person who has one friendship like that is richly blessed. A person who has many is blessed beyond measure. The important thing about friends is that they see you as you are and, for reasons most other people can't understand, they like you that way. The rest of the world does a pretty good job of telling us that we're not quite good enough, that we need more education, nicer clothes, more ambition and richer parents in order to be acceptable.

The rest of the world is wrong. What I need to be acceptable is to be accepted. That's the message the Bible says God sends to us—and, I think he sends that message through the people who like us just the way we are.

THINK

- What comes to mind when you think about friends you haven't seen or heard from in years?
- What are the most potent memories you have of old friendships?

- What is your response to the statement "A good friendship never disappears"?
- In what ways do your friends "see you as you are"? How do they demonstrate that they "like you that way"?
- How do good friendships enrich the way you understand God's relationship with you?

PRAY

God, show me how I can . . .

READ Betrayal and Forgiveness

From the ChristianityToday.com article "Why Friends Fail," by Les and Leslie Parrott[4]

When a once-trusted confidant double-crosses you, betrayal is the result. While change and neglect may be more common reasons for failed friendships, betrayal is almost always more painful. Why? Because betrayal dismantles trust. Your confidant, who knows your darkest secrets, . . . has let one of them out of the bag. After all, your close friend has the power to hurt you precisely because [he] knows you so well; your deepest secrets provide [him] with the emotional ammunition that can cut you to the core. You're left wondering if [he] will do it again.

Maybe your friend, whom you counted on, isn't there for you in a time of need. Or perhaps [he] joins others in teasing you about a sensitive issue. This brings up an important point: what we perceive as betrayal is often unintentional; your friend may not think what [he] did was wrong or realize that [he's] caused you pain. [He] may not have known you were counting on [him] so much. [He] may have thought you found [his] teasing funny, not hurtful. If your friend is acting out of anger or jealousy, however, and is thus seeking revenge, look out. You are now the victim of blatant betrayal. Whether intentional or not, betrayal is a guaranteed toxin to every friendship.

Matthew 18:21-35

At that point Peter got up the nerve to ask, "Master, how many times do I forgive a brother or sister who hurts me? Seven?"

Jesus replied, "Seven! Hardly. Try seventy times seven.

"The kingdom of God is like a king who decided to square accounts with his servants. As he got under way, one servant was brought before him who had run up a debt of a hundred thousand dollars. He couldn't pay up, so the king ordered the man, along with his wife, children, and goods, to be auctioned off at the slave market.

"The poor wretch threw himself at the king's feet and begged, 'Give me a chance and I'll pay it all back.' Touched by his plea, the king let him off, erasing the debt.

"The servant was no sooner out of the room when he came upon one of his fellow servants who owed him ten dollars. He seized him by the throat and demanded, 'Pay up. Now!'

"The poor wretch threw himself down and begged, 'Give me a chance and I'll pay it all back.' But he wouldn't do it. He had him arrested and put in jail until the debt was paid. When the other servants saw this going on, they were outraged and brought a detailed report to the king.

"The king summoned the man and said, 'You evil servant! I forgave your entire debt when you begged me for mercy. Shouldn't you be compelled to be merciful to your fellow servant who asked for mercy?' The king was furious and put the screws to the man until he paid back his entire debt. And that's exactly what my Father in heaven is going to do to each one of you who doesn't forgive unconditionally anyone who asks for mercy."

THINK

- What are examples of a friend who has betrayed you? (Be sensitive to the small-group members you may be discussing this with later. No fair naming names.) What about a time you betrayed a friend? (It's okay to name names here if you plan on asking forgiveness.)
- What betrayal risks do you face being in a small group like the one in which you'll (hopefully) go through this discussion guide?
- How much unease do you feel when telling a friend about your dark secrets? How do you feel when someone tells you about dark secrets?
- Betrayal—whether intentional or not—seems inevitable. How have you responded to past breaches of trust?

- What is the greatest challenge in forgiving a friend who stabs you in the back? Why try?
- The parable's message is pretty clear, but is it doable? How can you forgive unconditionally? How does that play out in real life?

PRAY

Father, give me wisdom to . . .

READ How to Be a Good Friend

Romans 12:9-16

Love from the center of who you are; don't fake it. Run for dear life from evil; hold on for dear life to good. Be good friends who love deeply; practice playing second fiddle.

Don't burn out; keep yourselves fueled and aflame. Be alert servants of the Master, cheerfully expectant. Don't quit in hard times; pray all the harder. Help needy Christians; be inventive in hospitality.

Bless your enemies; no cursing under your breath. Laugh with your happy friends when they're happy; share tears when they're down. Get along with each other; don't be stuck-up. Make friends with nobodies; don't be the great somebody.

THINK

- Why do you think Paul includes "practice playing second fiddle" in his description of being a good friend?
- What does it mean to "love deeply" in a friendship?
- When have you been "the great somebody" in a friendship? What did that do to the friendship?

PRAY

God, teach me the value of . . .

LIVE

What I Want to Discuss

What have you discovered this week that you definitely want to discuss with your small group? Write that here. Then begin your small-group discussion with these thoughts.

So What?

Use the following space to summarize the truths you uncovered about your accomplishments and what you really need to do to move out of a "treading water" mindset. Review your "Beginning Place" if you need to remember where you began. How does God's truth impact the "next step" in your journey?

Then What?

What is one practical thing you can do to apply what you've discovered? Describe how you would put this into practice. What steps would you take? Remember to think realistically—an admirable but unreachable goal is as good as no goal. Discuss your goal in your small group to further define it.

How?

Identify how you will be held accountable to the goal you described. Who will be on your support team? What are their responsibilities? How will you measure the success of your plan? Write the details here.

MY CHILDREN

"Parenting sometimes seems like a tireless exercise in frustration."

A REMINDER:

Before you dive into this study, spend a little time reviewing what you wrote in the previous lesson's "Live" sections. How are you doing? Check with your small-group members and review your progress toward the specified goals. If necessary, adjust your goals and plans, and then recommit to them.

THE BEGINNING PLACE

Ah, children. Aren't they great? They're cute, smart, funny, and a joy to be around. And then there's the other 1 to 99 percent of the time. If you haven't discovered it yet, there is no perfect child. (Well, maybe that one carpenter guy — but even he somehow forgot to tell his parents he had decided to stick around the temple a bit longer.) Perhaps you have a strong-willed

> **A note to men without children:** Wait! Come back! Don't skip this lesson. Much of what you'll discover in this exploration of dealing with children is applicable to other relationships, too. Think about it: What kids really want (love, affirmation, affection) is just what adults want. And much of what prompts a "treading water" attitude with children (frustration, poor communication, lack of respect) is not unlike what prompts the same attitude in other relationships. Whether you plan on having kids some day or not, work through this lesson.

five-year-old or a particularly fragile eleven-year-old. Maybe a teenager? An adult child? More than one?

Welcome to the wide world of uncertainty. Welcome to parenthood—a puzzle where the pieces are constantly changing and the box doesn't have a picture of the completed puzzle for easy reference. Nothing can truly prepare you for the challenges of parenting these uniquely created, uniquely flawed people—people who can seemingly simultaneously inspire and exasperate you. Children can make you feel proud one minute and like giving up the next.

Where are you right now in your relationships with your children? Are things going well? Are they completely out of control? Do you feel blessed to be a dad, or cursed? Use the space below to summarize your beginning place for this lesson. Describe your reality as well as your dreams. We'll start here and then go deeper.

READ Sometimes They Run Away

Luke 15:11-28

"There was once a man who had two sons. The younger said to his father, 'Father, I want right now what's coming to me.'

"So the father divided the property between them. It wasn't long before the younger son packed his bags and left for a distant country. There, undisciplined and dissipated, he wasted everything he had. After he had gone through all his money, there was a bad famine all through that country and he began to hurt. He signed on with a citizen there who assigned him to his fields to slop the pigs. He was so hungry he would have eaten the corncobs in the pig slop, but no one would give him any.

"That brought him to his senses. He said, 'All those farmhands working for my father sit down to three meals a day, and here I am starving to death. I'm going back to my father. I'll say to him, Father, I've sinned against God, I've sinned before you; I don't deserve to be called your son. Take me on as a hired hand.' He got right up and went home to his father.

"When he was still a long way off, his father saw him. His heart pounding, he ran out, embraced him, and kissed him. The son started his speech: 'Father, I've sinned against God, I've sinned before you; I don't deserve to be called your son ever again.'

"But the father wasn't listening. He was calling to the servants, 'Quick. Bring a clean set of clothes and dress him. Put the family ring on his finger and sandals on his feet. Then get a grain-fed heifer and roast it. We're going to feast! We're going to have a wonderful time! My son is here—given up for dead and now alive! Given up for lost and now found!' And they began to have a wonderful time.

"All this time his older son was out in the field. When the day's work was done he came in. As he approached the house, he heard the music and dancing. Calling over one of the houseboys, he asked what was going on. He told him, 'Your brother came home. Your father has ordered a feast—barbecued beef!—because he has him home safe and sound.'

"The older brother stalked off in an angry sulk and refused to join in. His father came out and tried to talk to him, but he wouldn't listen."

THINK

- What do you think the father was doing the whole time the younger son was away? How would you deal with a similar situation?
- What is the greatest challenge in parenting children who want everything "now"?
- Which of the two children in this story are you most like? Why? What implications might that have for the way you treat your children?
- What would be your greatest obstacles to absolute acceptance of a "prodigal" back into your home?

PRAY

Lord, help me overcome . . .

READ The Urge to Give Up

Hosea 11:1-9

"When Israel was only a child, I loved him.
    I called out, 'My son!'—called him out of Egypt.
But when others called him,
    he ran off and left me.
He worshiped the popular sex gods,
    he played at religion with toy gods.
Still, I stuck with him. I led Ephraim.
    I rescued him from human bondage,
But he never acknowledged my help,
    never admitted that I was the one pulling his wagon,
That I lifted him, like a baby, to my cheek,
    that I bent down to feed him.
Now he wants to go *back* to Egypt or go over to Assyria—
    anything but return to me!
That's why his cities are unsafe—the murder rate skyrockets
    and every plan to improve things falls to pieces.
My people are hell-bent on leaving me.
    They pray to god Baal for help.
    He doesn't lift a finger to help them.
But how can I give up on you, Ephraim?
    How can I turn you loose, Israel?
How can I leave you to be ruined like Admah,
    devastated like luckless Zeboim?
I can't bear to even think such thoughts.
    My insides churn in protest.
And so I'm not going to act on my anger.
    I'm not going to destroy Ephraim.
And why? Because I am God and not a human.
    I'm The Holy One and I'm here—in your very midst."

THINK

- When have you felt like giving up as a parent? What was your reaction to those feelings?
- How have you dealt with the frustration of children who don't obey?
- What actions or attitudes expressed by your children challenge your ability to be a good parent?
- How is God's relationship with Israel like your relationship with your children?
- God chose not to act on his anger against his "children" in this passage. Have you acted on your anger? What were the results of your anger? What would it take to act in a more loving way?
- What hope does this passage give about "hanging in there" with children who make parenting difficult?

PRAY

Father, give me the strength to . . .

READ A Tribe Apart

From *My Crazy Imperfect Christian Family*, by Glenn T. Stanton[1]

Several years ago, a television documentary and book came out looking at youth in America, drawing a frightening picture of parents in America. The documentary was done by the Public Broadcasting System, and it was called *The Lost Children of Rockdale County*. It began as a look at a syphilis outbreak in the spring of 1996 in Conyers, Georgia, an affluent suburb of Atlanta. As the crew's investigation unfolded, they found that the heart of the story wasn't the outbreak. It was how more than two hundred upper-middle-class teens contracted the disease.

These kids lived in beautiful homes and had all the material things teenagers could want. But their parents set almost no rules for them. The teens did drugs, drank, and had wild group-sex parties—all under the apathetic gaze of their parents. Some knew their kids were involved in such behavior and just couldn't muster the parental resolve to do anything, or they were just too busy making money for "stuff" to care. The cluelessness of these well-educated and professionally successful parents was stunning. They showed more intentionality in managing their retirement accounts than their children. The parents almost seemed like good actors playing bone-headed parents; you couldn't imagine real parents being this dense. But they were.

Another picture of parents was presented in a book by Patricia Hersch titled *A Tribe Apart: A Journey into the Heart of American Adolescence*. To research her book, Hersch entered the world of eight "average" middle-class adolescents in a Virginia town and lived among them for three years. She observed that these young people were "a tribe apart," not because they rebelled and separated themselves from the community, but because their parents neglected them—not materially, but parentally. Like the teens of Rockdale County, Georgia, these kids were adrift. . . .

These children are a new breed of orphan. They have biologically connected material-providers, but they don't have emotionally connected parents. They don't have mothers and fathers who make them feel like they matter. They don't have parents who set protective boundaries or ennobling expectations. They don't have parents who are emotionally nurturing or behaviorally directive. They don't have parents who strive to richly stock the wardrobe of their moral imaginations or deliberately work to develop the architecture of their characters. They don't have parents who love them with time and intimacy, rather than merely with stuff. They don't have parents who parent, for these are the primary deeds of parents.

Isaiah 58:7

What I'm interested in seeing you do is:
>   sharing your food with the hungry,
>   inviting the homeless poor into your homes,
>   putting clothes on the shivering ill-clad,
>   being available to your own families.

THINK

- Time for a gut check: In what ways have you withdrawn from your children? How much time do you actually spend with them?
- How do you make an emotional connection with your children? What clues do you get when you're not making that connection?
- What are the dangers of not taking the time to love your children with "time and intimacy"?
- What patterns in your life today suggest you might be creating "a tribe apart"? What will it take to change those patterns?
- How do you intentionally help your children feel as if they really matter?
- Describe what it means to "be available to your family." How are you doing this?

THINK (CONTINUED)

PRAY

God, show me how to reach out . . .

READ Whose Fault Is It Anyway?

Deuteronomy 11:2-9

Today it's very clear that it isn't your children who are front and center here: They weren't in on what GOD did, didn't see the acts, didn't experience the discipline, didn't marvel at his greatness, the way he displayed his power in the miracle-signs and deeds that he let loose in Egypt on Pharaoh king of Egypt and all his land, the way he took care of the Egyptian army, its horses and chariots, burying them in the waters of the Red Sea as they pursued you. GOD drowned them. And you're standing here today alive. Nor was it your children who saw how GOD took care of you in the wilderness up until the time you arrived here, what he did to Dathan and Abiram, the sons of Eliab son of Reuben, how the Earth opened its jaws and swallowed them with their families—their tents, and everything around them—right out of the middle of Israel. Yes, it was you—your eyes—that saw every great thing that GOD did.

So it's you who are in charge of keeping the entire commandment that I command you today so that you'll have the strength to invade and possess the land that you are crossing the river to make your own. Your obedience will give you a long life on the soil that GOD promised to give your ancestors and their children, a land flowing with milk and honey.

THINK

- In what ways have you suffered from your parents' mistakes? How might your children experience the impact of your poor choices?
- How easy or difficult is it to take responsibility for your role as a parent?
- What are the implications of this passage regarding the passing along of faith? What is the faith of your children? Do they see you as obedient to God?

- What is the potential impact of chastising a child for something he or she didn't know was wrong?
- This passage illustrates that parents and children are unique people. How does this truth affect the way you respond when children (particularly older children) rebel or make bad choices?

PRAY

Lord, help me set an example . . .

READ   Does It Really Matter?

From the *Psychology Today* article "The Daddy Dividend" [2]

Beyond birth and infancy, researchers are finding, a father's presence makes a big difference in a child's long-term development. Ross Parke, Ph.D., a psychologist at the University of California at Riverside, explains that children of involved fathers regulate their own emotions better.

They also have better social skills than children whose fathers are not involved in their lives and have better success in school. "It is clear that fathers affect their children's social, cognitive and emotional development," he says.

A father's influence seems to come, at least in part, through the unique ways that fathers play and interact with their children, says Kyle Pruett, M.D., a child psychiatrist at Yale. "Fathers are more likely to encourage their kids to tolerate frustration and master tasks on their own before they offer help," he explains, "whereas mothers tend to assist a fussing child earlier."

More than any particular social or cognitive skill, however, a father's love and affection may be the most significant gift he can give his children, says Ronald Rohner, Ph.D., a psychologist-anthropologist at the University of Connecticut, who for the past 40 years has been studying the effects of father love on children's development. "A father's love is often a significant buffer against depression, conduct problems and substance abuse," he finds.

"Children who experience their father's love are often more emotionally stable, less angry, have better self-esteem and have a more positive worldview," Rohner says, To his surprise, he discovered that "father love is often as influential as mother love on a child's happiness and sense of well-being."

THINK

- Are there times when you feel that your role as a father is somehow less important than that of a mother? What prompts those feelings?
- How is the way you interact with your children different from the way their mother interacts? How does that support the claims of the *Psychology Today* article?
- What form does your "love and affection" take with your children?
- What (if any) changes should you make in your relationship with your children to positively influence their happiness and well-being?

PRAY

God, help me see my role as . . .

READ The Power of Love

Ephesians 4:32–5:2

> Be gentle with one another, sensitive. Forgive one another as quickly and thoroughly as God in Christ forgave you.
>
> Watch what God does, and then you do it, like children who learn proper behavior from their parents. Mostly what God does is love you. Keep company with him and learn a life of love. Observe how Christ loved us. His love was not cautious but extravagant. He didn't love in order to get something from us but to give everything of himself to us. Love like that.

Proverbs 22:1-6

> A sterling reputation is better than striking it rich;
>> a gracious spirit is better than money in the bank.
>
> The rich and the poor shake hands as equals—
>> GOD made them both!
>
> A prudent person sees trouble coming and ducks;
>> a simpleton walks in blindly and is clobbered.
>
> The payoff for meekness and Fear-of-GOD
>> is plenty and honor and a satisfying life.
>
> The perverse travel a dangerous road, potholed and mud-slick;
>> if you know what's good for you, stay clear of it.
>
> Point your kids in the right direction—
>> when they're old they won't be lost.

THINK

- In what ways have you shown gentleness or sensitivity toward your children? How easy or difficult is that?
- Respond to the statement "Mostly what God does is love you" in the context of how you relate to your children. Will your children

say, "Mostly what Dad does is love us"? Why or why not?

- What does it mean to have extravagant love for your children? How well do you do this?

- The "point your kids" proverb can seem simplistic and trite when set apart. In the context of the previous verses, what can you learn about the role of diligence in helping your kids discover truth?

- How do you reconcile this proverb with times when your children do seem to get lost even though you've been a diligent "direction pointer"?

PRAY

God, teach me to love . . .

READ What's Missing?

From *Guard Your Heart*, by Gary Rosberg[3]

I was sitting in my favorite chair, studying for the final stages of my doctoral degree, when Sarah announced herself in my presence with a question: "Daddy, do you want to see my family picture?"

"Sarah, Daddy's busy. Come back in a little while, honey."

Good move, right? I was busy. A week's worth of work to squeeze into a weekend. You've been there.

Ten minutes later she swept back into the living room. "Daddy, let me show you my picture."

The heat went up around my collar. "Sarah, I said come back later. This is important."

Three minutes later she stormed into the living room, got three inches from my nose, and barked with all the power a five-year-old could muster: "Do you want to see it or don't you?" The assertive Christian woman in training.

"No," I told her, "I don't."

With that she zoomed out of the room and left me alone. And somehow, being alone at that moment wasn't as satisfying as I thought it would be. I felt like a jerk. (Don't agree so loudly.) I went to the front door.

"Sarah," I called, "could you come back inside a minute, please? Daddy would like to see your picture."

She obliged with no recriminations and popped up on my lap.

It was a great picture. She'd even given it a title. Across the top, in her best printing, she had inscribed: "OUR FAMILY BEST."

"Tell me about it," I said.

"Here is Mommy [a stick figure with long yellow curly hair], here is me standing by Mommy [with a smiley face], here is our dog Katie, and here is Missy [her little sister was a stick figure lying in the street in front of the house, about three times bigger than anyone else]." It was a pretty good insight into how she saw our family.

"I love your picture, honey," I told her. "I'll hang it on the dining-room wall, and each night when I come home from work and from class, I'm going to look at it."

She took me at my word, beamed ear to ear, and went outside to play. I went back to my books. But for some reason I kept reading the same paragraph over and over.

Something was making me uneasy.

Something about Sarah's picture.

Something was missing.

I went to the front door. "Sarah," I called, "could you come back inside a minute, please? I want to look at your picture again, honey."

Sarah crawled back into my lap. I can close my eyes right now and see the way she looked. Cheeks rosy from playing outside. Pigtails. Strawberry Shortcake tennis shoes. A Cabbage Patch doll named Nellie tucked limply under her arm.

I asked my little girl a question, but I wasn't sure I wanted to hear the answer.

"Honey . . . there's Mommy, and Sarah, and Missy. Katie the dog is in the picture, and the sun, and the house, and squirrels, and birdies. But Sarah . . . where is your Daddy?"

"You're at the library," she said.

With that simple statement my little princess stopped time for me. Lifting her gently off my lap, I sent her back to play in the spring sunshine. I slumped back in my chair with a swirling head and blood pumping furiously through my heart. Even as I type these words into the computer, I can feel those sensations all over again. It was a frightening moment. The fog lifted from my preoccupied brain for a moment—and suddenly I could see. But what I saw scared me to death. It was like being in a ship and coming out of the fog in time to see a huge, sharp rock knifing through the surf just off the port bow.

Sarah's simple pronouncement—"You're at the library"—got my attention big-time. I resolved right then to change—to be a daddy who was there for his kids, who didn't spend every moment studying or at the office, who was an active participant in his children's lives. Sure, it might slow down my career ambitions a bit. But I desperately wanted my daughter to know that she was the pride and joy of my life—and that she could show me her latest drawing anytime.

It was time for this daddy to get back in the picture.

THINK

- Where (if at all) do you see yourself in this story?
- What impacted you most about this story?
- In what ways are you "out of the picture" with your children?
- How can you get back into the picture?
- What does this story tell you about the importance of "being there" for your kids?

PRAY

Father, help me to "be there" . . .

LIVE

What I Want to Discuss

What have you discovered this week that you definitely want to discuss with your small group? Write that here. Then begin your small-group discussion with these thoughts.

So What?

Use the following space to summarize the truths you uncovered about your accomplishments and what you really need to do to move out of a "treading water" mindset. Review your "Beginning Place" if you need to remember where you began. How does God's truth impact the "next step" in your journey?

Then What?

What is one practical thing you can do to apply what you've discovered? Describe how you would put this into practice. What steps would you take? Remember to think realistically—an admirable but unreachable goal is as good as no goal. Discuss your goal in your small group to further define it.

How?

Identify how you will be held accountable to the goal you described. Who will be on your support team? What are their responsibilities? How will you measure the success of your plan? Write the details here.

MY
WIFE

"My wife isn't the person I married."

A REMINDER:

Before you dive into this study, spend a little time reviewing what you wrote in the previous lesson's "Live" sections. How are you doing? Check with your small-group members and review your progress toward the specified goals. If necessary, adjust your goals and plans, and then recommit to them.

THE BEGINNING PLACE

First question: Do you love your wife?

The easy answer (and the "right thing to say") is "yes." Of course you love your wife. After all, you married her, right? You made a commitment. That means something. Doesn't it?

Love is a tricky thing. Sometimes you "feel" it. Other times you count on just knowing it. But there is something foundational about it— something that gives it significance no matter what the life circumstance.

A note to unmarried men: We understand that not everyone who reads this is married. And while it would be nice to promise that you'll still get lots of good stuff out of this lesson, that would be a bit naïve. We certainly hope you learn some valuable info (wisdom that could improve your current or future relationship with a girlfriend or future spouse). But it is also possible the topic won't be directly applicable to your life. Nevertheless, please don't skip over this lesson. The perspective you bring to a small-group discussion may be just what someone else in the group needs to hear. Think about the readings and make notes as usual, considering how you think they might apply to marriage (or what you've observed in others' marriages).

Second question: Do you like your wife?

"Sure." "Of course." "Most of the time." "Well . . . we get along okay."

Ah, this one is stickier. While we can always fall back on "I love you" as a foundational truth, the "like" part isn't always so easy to believe. That's because people change. The beauty queen you courted in high school can't fit into the prom dress. Her once-cute laugh lines suddenly look like (gasp) age lines. She doesn't greet you with a passion-drenched kiss anymore. She's stressed by work, kids, and bills that scream to be paid. She's even impatient with your once-adorable ability to burp the alphabet.

And let's not even get started on you. You've changed, too.

So what do you do? How do you move through married life when married life looks completely different from what you once knew or hoped for?

Dig around until you have a good starting place for this lesson. Be honest about the good, the bad, and the ugly aspects of your relationship with your wife. How has your marriage lived up to your expectations? In what ways is it the manifestation of the ideal you once believed? And what about sex? Infidelity? Intimacy? What's really going on? Make note of the good—be generous with the good stuff—but don't ignore the things that frustrate you or bring you down. Keep in mind this is not a "gripe" session. Our focus will be on expectations, reality, and how to rediscover hope and wonder in your relationship with your wife.

Use the space below to summarize your beginning place for this lesson. Describe your spousal realities as well as your dreams. We'll start here and then go deeper.

READ The Honeymoon's Over

From "Incompatibility," a BacktotheBible.org interview with Elisabeth Elliot[1]

Whenever you hear anybody explain why they got a divorce, it seems as though in every case they say, "Well, we've grown apart. She is not the woman I married. I'm not the woman who married him. He is not the man I married. We've changed so much."

Well, I want to say, "So what else is new? What did you think you were getting? If you're marrying a real live human being, there will be many changes and there are going to be many revelations and there are going to be many revolutions in your life, if you're going to make it work out."

We can't know the cost in advance. We are all, let's face it, incompatible.

Luke 6:32-33

"If you only love the lovable, do you expect a pat on the back? Run-of-the-mill sinners do that. If you only help those who help you, do you expect a medal? Garden-variety sinners do that."

THINK

- What are the clues that a husband and wife have "grown apart"?
- How have you changed in terms of your relationship with your wife? How has she changed?
- What is the greatest challenge in maintaining a marriage in which both partners have changed since the wedding?
- In what ways are you and your wife incompatible? How do you deal with these realities?
- In what ways were your marriage expectations realistic? Unrealistic?
- What does it mean to love the "unlovable" in the context of marriage? In the context of your marriage?

THINK (CONTINUED)

PRAY

Lord, shape my expectations in . . .

READ Suddenly Lost

From the play *Dinner with Friends*, by Donald Margulies[2]

In this scene from the award-winning play, Gabe is attempting to interpret the dream his wife, Karen, keeps having. He tells her he believes the dream is about what happens to couples over time—what he calls an "inevitable evolution."

GABE:	Okay. (A beat) It's . . . I think it's what happens when . . . when practical matters begin to outweigh . . . abandon. You know?
KAREN:	Abandon?
GABE:	Uh-huh.
KAREN:	Is that it?

(Gabe nods)

	Do they have to?
GABE:	I think so. (A beat) I think so.
KAREN:	Why?
GABE:	(Shrugs) It's . . . I think it is . . . You know: having kids . . . having to pay the mortgage . . . making the deadline . . . marinating the snapper . . .
KAREN:	(Tears in her eyes) Don't you ever miss me, Gabe?
GABE:	(Surprised by her sudden emotion) What?
KAREN:	Don't you ever miss me?
GABE:	O, God, honey, yes. Yes. Sure I miss you. I miss you a lot.
KAREN:	(Almost childlike) How do we not get lost?

THINK

- In what ways do you "miss" your wife? How might she "miss" you?
- How have practical matters outweighed abandon in your relationship? Is it inevitable in a marriage? What can you do to recover some of the abandon?

• What does it take to keep from "getting lost" in a marriage relationship?

PRAY

God, help me not to miss . . .

READ It's All About Sex

From *The Sex-Starved Marriage*, by Michele Weiner Davis[3]

Dear Michele,

Please, please help me. I am going through hell!! I am twenty-eight years old, married with a three-year-old daughter. For the past three years, my wife has avoided being sexual with me. It has slowly gone from having sex maybe twice a week to now, if I'm lucky, once a month. And even then, it's not really having sex. It's more like her saying, "Hurry up and get in here, and let's do this before our child wakes up." There is no foreplay. She doesn't even kiss me. I'm the one who always is initiating any sort of affection.

I get completely angered, hurt, and resentful toward her because I can't understand how she could be so cruel to me. I want to tell her, "If you don't love me anymore, then we can split up and move on," but we have a child together, and I don't think that's right or fair to our daughter. I want to be there when my little girl wakes up in the morning and goes to bed at night. But I also don't want to be with a woman who doesn't want to be with me.

So I struggle every day with what I should do because I can't keep living like this. I'm miserable. I have talked to my wife about how I feel numerous times, and nothing I say seems to change anything. Is there anything else I can do besides getting a divorce? Is there something you could write to her so she hears from another person about the importance of a good sexual relationship in a marriage?

Does any of this sound familiar? Are these things you've thought or said to yourself? Or have you heard words like these uttered from your spouse in an attempt to get *you* to change? Either way, you need to know that you are not alone. It is estimated that one out of every three couples struggle with problems associated with low sexual desire. One study found that 20 percent of married couples have sex fewer than ten times a year! Complaints about low desire are the #1 problem brought to sex therapists.

And if you've been thinking that low sexual desire is only "a woman's thing," think again. Many sex experts believe that low sexual desire in men is America's best-kept secret. . . .

Contrary to what you might be thinking, saying a marriage is sex starved tells you virtually nothing about how much or how little sex a couple is actually having. It's not about numbers. It's not just about sexless couples who have slept in separate bedrooms for years. In fact, it includes couples who, according to national surveys, have an "average" amount of sex each month. Since, unlike vitamins, there are no recommended daily requirements to ensure a healthy sex life, a sex-starved marriage is more about the fallout that occurs when one spouse is deeply unhappy with his or her sexual relationship and this unhappiness is ignored, minimized, or dismissed. The resulting disintegration of the relationship encapsulates the real meaning of a sex-starved marriage.

Sex is an extremely important part of marriage. When it's good, it offers couples opportunities to give and receive physical pleasure, to connect emotionally and spiritually. It builds closeness, intimacy, and a sense of partnership. It defines their relationship as different from all others. Sex is a powerful tie that binds.

THINK

- On a scale of one to ten, with one being "not at all" and ten being "more than you know," how important is the sexual component in your marriage? How might your wife rate this?
- What are the implications of differing scores in the question above?
- How comfortable are you in talking about sex with your wife? Explain your answer.
- Why does the issue of sex often lead to resentment in a marriage relationship?

- Respond to the following statement: "There are no recommended daily requirements to ensure a healthy sex life."
- What challenges do you face in trying to find a healthy, balanced sex life?

PRAY

God, show me how to avoid . . .

READ It's Still About Sex

From the MarriagePartnership.com article "What Does the Bible Say?" by Steve Tracy[4]

Scripture doesn't picture marital union without physical union. The beautiful erotic imagery of Genesis 2:24-25 is unambiguous. Marriage is a "one flesh" relationship. Sex is not peripheral to marriage but is delicately woven into its very fabric.

Sexual union expresses, reinforces, and reenacts the marital covenant itself. This helps to explain the Hebrew euphemism for marital sex—"to know." Adam, who'd been given Eve as his life companion on the sixth day of Creation, could continue to express and reenact their union throughout their earthly days by "knowing" Eve sexually (Genesis 4:1). Even the apostle Paul, who championed singleness, said that sex is so essential to marriage that withholding it is "to defraud" or steal from one's spouse (1 Corinthians 7:3-5). This doesn't mean you should have sex every time you don't feel like it, or that you should merely go through the motions to keep peace. But it does mean you'll take sex seriously as one of many vital ingredients in a healthy marriage.

Sex doesn't create marriage, but sex cannot be divorced from marriage. The gracious God who created marriage would have it no other way.

1 Corinthians 6:16-20

There's more to sex than mere skin on skin. Sex is as much spiritual mystery as physical fact. As written in Scripture, "The two become one." Since we want to become spiritually one with the Master, we must not pursue the kind of sex that avoids commitment and intimacy, leaving us more lonely than ever—the kind of sex that can never "become one." There is a sense in which sexual sins are different from all others. In sexual sin we violate the sacredness of our own bodies, these bodies that were made for God-given and God-modeled love, for "becoming one" with another. Or didn't you realize that your body is a sacred place, the place of the Holy Spirit? Don't you see that you can't live however you please, squandering what God paid such a high price for? The physical part of you is not some piece of property belonging to the spiritual part of you. God owns the whole works. So let people see God in and through your body.

1 Corinthians 7:1-6

Now, getting down to the questions you asked in your letter to me. First, Is it a good thing to have sexual relations?

Certainly—but only within a certain context. It's good for a man to have a wife, and for a woman to have a husband. Sexual drives are strong, but marriage is strong enough to contain them and provide for a balanced and fulfilling sexual life in a world of sexual disorder. The marriage bed must be a place of mutuality— the husband seeking to satisfy his wife, the wife seeking to satisfy her husband. Marriage is not a place to "stand up for your rights." Marriage is a decision to serve the other, whether in bed or out. Abstaining from sex is permissible for a period of time if you both agree to it, and if it's for the purposes of prayer and fasting—but only for such times. Then come back together again. Satan has an ingenious way of tempting us when we least expect it. I'm not, understand, commanding these periods of abstinence—only providing my best counsel if you should choose them.

THINK

- Scripture seems to indicate that sex is an important part of the marriage relationship. What do you think about this?
- What does it mean that sex is more than "skin on skin"? What does the spiritual aspect of sex look like to you? To your wife?
- Do you agree with Paul's assertion that sexual sins are different from all others? Why or why not?
- What did Paul mean when he said that "the marriage bed must be a place of mutuality"?

- What does serving one another "whether in bed or out" mean in practical terms? How well are you doing that?
- Do you and your wife ever abstain from sex "for the purposes of prayer and fasting"? For other reasons? Is this something you'd like to change?

PRAY

Lord, guide me in my marriage by . . .

READ Still in Love?

From *The Four Loves*, by C. S. Lewis[5]

By Eros I mean of course that state which we call "being in love"; or, if you prefer, that kind of love which lovers are "in." . . .

The carnal or animally sexual element within Eros, I intend (following an old usage) to call Venus. . . .

Can we be in this selfless liberation for a lifetime? Hardly for a week. Between the best possible lovers this high condition is intermittent. The old self soon turns out to be not so dead as he pretended—as after a religious conversion. In either he may be momentarily knocked flat; he will soon be up again; if not on his feet at least on his elbow, if not roaring, at least back to his surly grumbling or his mendicant whine. And Venus will often slip back into more sexuality.

But these lapses will not destroy a marriage between two "decent and sensible" people. The couple whose marriage will certainly be endangered by them, and possibly ruined, are those who have idolised Eros. They thought he had the power and truthfulness of a god. They expected that mere feeling would do for them, and permanently, all that was necessary. When this expectation is disappointed they throw the blame on Eros or, more usually, on their partners. In reality, however, Eros, having made his gigantic promise and shown you in glimpses what its performance would be like, has "done his stuff." He, like a god-parent, makes the vows; it is we who must keep them. It is we who must labour to bring our daily life into even closer accordance with what the glimpses have revealed. We must do the works of Eros when Eros is not present. This all good lovers know, though those who are not reflective or articulate will be able to express it only in a few conventional phrases about "taking the rough along with the smooth," "not expecting too much," having "a little common sense," and the like. And all good Christian lovers know that this programme, modest as it sounds, will not be carried out except by humility, charity and divine grace; that it is indeed the whole Christian life seen from one particular angle.

THINK

- What does it really mean to "be in love"?
- What is your reaction to the claim that being in love is an "intermittent" condition?
- In what ways has an idolization of sex damaged marriages?
- Is there a difference between "having sex" and "making love"?
- How is it possible to "bring our daily life into even closer accordance with what the glimpses have revealed"?

PRAY

Father, teach me how to love . . .

READ Emotional Infidelity

From the *USA Today* article "Infidelity Reaches Beyond Having Sex," by Karen S. Peterson[6]

Cybersex and so-called virtual affairs on the Internet are all the buzz among professionals who study spouses who stray.

But the truly fertile ground for dangerous emotional attachments outside marriages is much more conventional: the workplace. As more employees labor longer hours together, close friendships increasingly are taken for granted. And as more women move into professions once dominated by men, there are greater temptations for both sexes.

There is a new "crisis of infidelity" breeding in the workplace, says Baltimore psychologist and marital researcher Shirley Glass. Often it does not involve sexual thrill seekers, but "good people," peers who are in good marriages.

"The new infidelity is between people who unwittingly form deep, passionate connections before realizing that they've crossed the line from platonic friendship into romantic love," Glass says.

Glass' 25 years of research on "extramarital attachments" adds to a growing understanding of just what constitutes infidelity and why it happens.

She believes affairs do not have to include sex. "In the new infidelity, affairs do not have to be sexual. Sometimes the greatest betrayals happen without touching. Infidelity is any emotional or sexual intimacy that violates trust."

This revised concept of an affair is embraced by increasing numbers of Glass' colleagues. People are "incredibly devastated by their partner's emotional affair," says Peggy Vaughan, who has researched infidelity for 20 years. "They separate over it, divorce over it, this breaking of a trust, a bond."

A platonic friendship, such as those that grow at work, edges into an emotional affair when three elements are present, Glass says:

- Emotional intimacy. Transgressors share more of their "inner

self, frustrations and triumphs than with their spouses.
They are on a slippery slope when they begin sharing the
dissatisfaction with their marriage with a co-worker."

- Secrecy and deception. "They neglect to say, 'We meet
  every morning for coffee.' Once the lying starts, the intimacy shifts farther away from the marriage."
- Sexual chemistry. Even though the two may not act on the
  chemistry, there is at least an unacknowledged sexual
  attraction.

Malachi 2:13-16

You fill the place of worship with your whining and sniveling
because you don't get what you want from GOD. Do you know
why? Simple. Because GOD was there as a witness when you
spoke your marriage vows to your young bride, and now you've
broken those vows, broken the faith-bond with your vowed
companion, your covenant wife. GOD, not you, made marriage.
His Spirit inhabits even the smallest details of marriage. And
what does he want from marriage? Children of God, that's what.
So guard the spirit of marriage within you. Don't cheat on your
spouse.

"I hate divorce," says the GOD of Israel. GOD-of-the-Angel-
Armies says, "I hate the violent dismembering of the 'one flesh'
of marriage." So watch yourselves. Don't let your guard down.
Don't cheat.

THINK

- Why is the workplace a breeding ground for "dangerous emotional attachments"?
- What is your response to the proposition that affairs don't have
  to include sex?
- Be honest: Have you ever had an emotional affair or been
  close to one?

- Which of the three elements (emotional intimacy, secrecy and deception, and sexual chemistry) are you most susceptible to? How can you confront each of these so they don't damage your marriage?
- What is your level of vulnerability to these types of situations? What are the practical reasons for that? What can you do to lower the level of vulnerability?
- Malachi's blunt comments about marriage were included in the larger context of broken covenants with God. Why is it significant that he references the marriage covenant as an example of this? How does it fit with the previous article?

PRAY

God, help me stay strong when . . .

READ Unpacking Some Expectations

Ephesians 5:21-33

> Out of respect for Christ, be courteously reverent to one another.
>
> Wives, understand and support your husbands in ways that show your support for Christ. The husband provides leadership to his wife the way Christ does to his church, not by domineering but by cherishing. So just as the church submits to Christ as he exercises such leadership, wives should likewise submit to their husbands.
>
> Husbands, go all out in your love for your wives, exactly as Christ did for the church—a love marked by giving, not getting. Christ's love makes the church whole. His words evoke her beauty. Everything he does and says is designed to bring the best out of her, dressing her in dazzling white silk, radiant with holiness. And that is how husbands ought to love their wives. They're really doing themselves a favor—since they're already "one" in marriage.
>
> No one abuses his own body, does he? No, he feeds and pampers it. That's how Christ treats us, the church, since we are part of his body. And this is why a man leaves father and mother and cherishes his wife. No longer two, they become "one flesh." This is a huge mystery, and I don't pretend to understand it all. What is clearest to me is the way Christ treats the church. And this provides a good picture of how each husband is to treat his wife, loving himself in loving her, and how each wife is to honor her husband.

THINK

- How are you "courteously reverent" to your wife? What does that look like?
- In what ways do you "go all out in your love" for your wife? In what ways do you hold back?
- What does it look like to do and say things that "bring the best out" of your wife? How often do you instead bring out the worst? How do you change that?

- In practical terms, how can you "cherish your wife"?
- How does loving your wife help you to love yourself? How does that love move you out of a "treading water" mentality?

PRAY

Lord, show me how to cherish . . .

LIVE

What I Want to Discuss

What have you discovered this week that you definitely want to discuss with your small group? Write that here. Then begin your small-group discussion with these thoughts.

So What?

Use the following space to summarize the truths you uncovered about your accomplishments and what you really need to do to move out of a "treading water" mindset. Review your "Beginning Place" if you need to remember where you began. How does God's truth impact the "next step" in your journey?

Then What?

What is one practical thing you can do to apply what you've discovered? Describe how you would put this into practice. What steps would you take? Remember to think realistically—an admirable but unreachable goal is as good as no goal. Discuss your goal in your small group to further define it.

How?

Identify how you will be held accountable to the goal you described. Who will be on your support team? What are their responsibilities? How will you measure the success of your plan? Write the details here.

MY
FAITH

"My faith is stuck in a rut; it feels stale."

A REMINDER:

Before you dive into this study, spend a little time reviewing what you wrote in the previous lesson's "Live" sections. How are you doing? Check with your small-group members and review your progress toward the specified goals. If necessary, adjust your goals and plans, and then recommit to them.

THE BEGINNING PLACE

In the first days of a newfound faith, life is often defined by a world of possibilities. There is so much to learn, so much to experience, and so much to discover about this "life of faith." In time, we become less excited and more practical about what it means to be a Christian. We spend more time on the immediate demands—children, family, friends, career—and less time on things that don't seem to have immediate consequences. It's a natural progression for many men, but it can lead to seasons—some quite long—when the faith life doesn't feel at all fresh, relevant, or worth pursuing with anything other than casual effort.

It is in these times that we lose the point. We lose sight of what it was that brought us into a relationship with Christ in the first place—Jesus' ultimate sacrifice, the unwarranted yet unbelievable gift of grace, and love so real you could taste it.

Perhaps it is naïve to expect your maturing faith would look anything like that first encounter. Certainly the reality of everyday life (and reality's ugly cousin, cynicism) temper the sense of wonder. So how do you recapture the awe? How do you bring back the meaning of faith?

You begin with where you are. What does your faith life look like today? How has it changed? If you feel "stuck," what brought you to that place? What kind of a faith do you long for?

Use the space below to summarize your beginning place for this lesson. Describe your reality as well as your dreams. We'll start here and then go deeper.

READ Not Yet Perfect

Galatians 2:16-21

We know very well that we are not set right with God by rule-keeping but only through personal faith in Jesus Christ. How do we know? We tried it—and we had the best system of rules the world has ever seen! Convinced that no human being can please God by self-improvement, we believed in Jesus as the Messiah so that we might be set right before God by trusting in the Messiah, not by trying to be good.

Have some of you noticed that we are not yet perfect? (No great surprise, right?) And are you ready to make the accusation that since people like me, who go through Christ in order to get things right with God, aren't perfectly virtuous, Christ must therefore be an accessory to sin? The accusation is frivolous. If I was "trying to be good," I would be rebuilding the same old barn that I tore down. I would be acting as a charlatan.

What actually took place is this: I tried keeping rules and working my head off to please God, and it didn't work. So I quit being a "law man" so that I could be *God's* man. Christ's life showed me how, and enabled me to do it. I identified myself completely with him. Indeed, I have been crucified with Christ. My ego is no longer central. It is no longer important that I appear righteous before you or have your good opinion, and I am no longer driven to impress God. Christ lives in me. The life you see me living is not "mine," but it is lived by faith in the Son of God, who loved me and gave himself for me. I am not going to go back on that.

Is it not clear to you that to go back to that old rule-keeping, peer-pleasing religion would be an abandonment of everything personal and free in my relationship with God? I refuse to do that, to repudiate God's grace. If a living relationship with God could come by rule-keeping, then Christ died unnecessarily.

THINK

- In what ways have you tried to grow your faith by "rule-keeping"?
- What's so wrong about trying to be good?
- Has "rule-keeping" ever led you to a feeling that your faith is stuck in a rut?
- If "rule-keeping" is an obstacle to faith, how do you overcome that obstacle? How do you move from being a "law man" to being "God's man"?

PRAY

God, help me to avoid . . .

READ To Please or To Trust

From *TrueFaced*, by Bill Thrall, Bruce McNicol, and John Lynch[1]

Pleasing God is an incredibly good longing. It always will be. But it can't be our primary motivation, or it will imprison our hearts. *Pleasing is not a means to our personal godliness, it is the fruit of our godliness for it is the fruit of trust. We will never please God through our efforts to become godly. Rather, we will only please God—and become godly—when we trust God.* If we strive to please God by solving our sin, we are back at the same insufficient square one that put us in need of a savior. And we are stuck with our talents, skill, desire, ability, longing, chutzpah, diligence, and resolve to make it happen. Now we've got habañera sauce on our cornflakes.

What value, then, flows from the motive of Trusting God? When our motive is Trusting God, our value will be Living Out of Who God Says I Am. Have we already been changed? Yes. As day is from night, we have changed. We have received a new heart, for crying out loud! We have a brand-new core identity. We have already been changed, and now we get to mature into who we already are.

THINK

- How do you experience the longing to please God?
- Is it wrong to try to solve your sin? Why or why not?
- What motive drives your faith life: the desire to please God or the desire to trust him?
- Practically speaking, what does it mean that you have a "new core identity"?
- What is the greatest risk of trusting God?

THINK (CONTINUED)

PRAY

Lord, teach me to trust . . .

READ Living What You're Saying

Matthew 7:13-29

"Don't look for shortcuts to God. The market is flooded with surefire, easygoing formulas for a successful life that can be practiced in your spare time. Don't fall for that stuff, even though crowds of people do. The way to life—to God!—is vigorous and requires total attention.

"Be wary of false preachers who smile a lot, dripping with practiced sincerity. Chances are they are out to rip you off some way or other. Don't be impressed with charisma; look for character. Who preachers *are* is the main thing, not what they say. A genuine leader will never exploit your emotions or your pocketbook. These diseased trees with their bad apples are going to be chopped down and burned.

"Knowing the correct password—saying 'Master, Master,' for instance—isn't going to get you anywhere with me. What is required is serious obedience—*doing* what my Father wills. I can see it now—at the Final Judgment thousands strutting up to me and saying, 'Master, we preached the Message, we bashed the demons, our God-sponsored projects had everyone talking.' And do you know what I am going to say? 'You missed the boat. All you did was use me to make yourselves important. You don't impress me one bit. You're out of here.'

"These words I speak to you are not incidental additions to your life, homeowner improvements to your standard of living. They are foundational words, words to build a life on. If you work these words into your life, you are like a smart carpenter who built his house on solid rock. Rain poured down, the river flooded, a tornado hit—but nothing moved that house. It was fixed to the rock.

"But if you just use my words in Bible studies and don't work them into your life, you are like a stupid carpenter who built his house on the sandy beach. When a storm rolled in and the waves came up, it collapsed like a house of cards."

When Jesus concluded his address, the crowd burst into applause. They had never heard teaching like this. It was apparent that he was living everything he was saying—quite a contrast to their religion teachers! This was the best teaching they had ever heard.

THINK

- In contrast with previous readings, this passage suggests that the way to God is vigorous, and not merely living by faith and trust. How do you reconcile these ideas?
- Who are the "false preachers" in your world today?
- How do you express "serious obedience"? What makes that difficult?
- How might using Jesus' words without working them into your life lead to a stalled faith life?
- In what ways are you living what you're saying? Where is there disconnect between your words and actions?

PRAY

Father, may my words and actions . . .

READ   Responsibility

From *The Pursuit of Holiness*, by Jerry Bridges[2]

During a certain period in my Christian life, I thought that any effort on my part to live a holy life was "of the flesh" and that "the flesh profits for nothing." I thought God would not bless any effort on my part to live the Christian life, just as He would not bless any effort on my part to become a Christian by good works. Just as I received Christ Jesus by faith, so I was to seek a holy life only by faith. Any effort on my part was just getting in God's way. I misapplied the statement, "You will not have to fight this battle. Take up your positions; stand firm and see the deliverance the Lord will give you" (2 Chronicles 20:17), to mean that I was just to turn it all over to the Lord and He would fight the sin in my life. In fact, in the margin of the Bible I was using during that period I wrote alongside the verse these words: "Illustration of walking in the Spirit."

How foolish I was. I misconstrued dependence on the Holy Spirit to mean I was to make no effort, that I had no responsibility. I mistakenly thought if I turned it all over to the Lord, He would make my choices for me and would choose obedience over disobedience. All I needed was to look to Him for holiness. But this is not God's way. He makes provision for our holiness, but He gives us the responsibility of using those provisions.

THINK

- What is the difference between dependence on the Holy Spirit and taking responsibility to seek holiness?
- When have you felt you ought to seek a holy life "only by faith"?
- Have you ever felt that the best approach to faith is to offer no effort of your own? What is the result of this approach?
- What does it mean that God gives us the responsibility to use the provisions he's given us? Are you generally doing that?

THINK (CONTINUED)

PRAY

God, teach me responsibility . . .

READ Guest List

Psalm 15:1-5

GOD, who gets invited
>   to dinner at your place?
How do we get on your guest list?

"Walk straight,
>   act right,
>   tell the truth.

"Don't hurt your friend,
>   don't blame your neighbor;
>   despise the despicable.

"Keep your word even when it costs you,
>   make an honest living,
>   never take a bribe.

"You'll never get
blacklisted
if you live like this."

Luke 13:23-30

A bystander said, "Master, will only a few be saved?"

He said, "Whether few or many is none of your business. Put your mind on your life with God. The way to life—to God!—is vigorous and requires your total attention. A lot of you are going to assume that you'll sit down to God's salvation banquet just because you've been hanging around the neighborhood all your lives. Well, one day you're going to be banging on the door, wanting to get in, but you'll find the door locked and the Master saying, 'Sorry, you're not on my guest list.'

"You'll protest, 'But we've known you all our lives!' only to be interrupted with his abrupt, 'Your kind of knowing can hardly be called knowing. You don't know the first thing about me.'

"That's when you'll find yourselves out in the cold, strangers to grace. You'll watch Abraham, Isaac, Jacob, and all the prophets march into God's kingdom. You'll watch outsiders stream in from east, west, north, and south and sit down at the table of God's kingdom. And all the time you'll be outside looking in—and wondering what happened. This is the Great Reversal: the last in line put at the head of the line, and the so-called first ending up last."

THINK

- What do these passages say about what God really wants from you?
- Are you sure you're on God's guest list? Why or why not?
- In what ways can "your kind of knowing . . . hardly be called knowing"?
- How do you truly get to know God?
- What do these passages tell you about the role of humility in faith? The role of diligence?

PRAY

Lord, show me what you really want . . .

READ Failed Attempts

Psalm 32:1-11

Count yourself lucky, how happy you must be—
>   you get a fresh start,
>   your slate's wiped clean.

Count yourself lucky—
>   GOD holds nothing against you
>   and you're holding nothing back from him.

When I kept it all inside,
>   my bones turned to powder,
>   my words became daylong groans.

The pressure never let up;
>   all the juices of my life dried up.

Then I let it all out;
>   I said, "I'll make a clean breast of my failures to GOD."

Suddenly the pressure was gone—
>   my guilt dissolved,
>   my sin disappeared.

These things add up. Every one of us needs to pray;
>   when all hell breaks loose and the dam bursts
>   we'll be on high ground, untouched.

GOD's my island hideaway,
>   keeps danger far from the shore,
>   throws garlands of hosannas around my neck.

Let me give you some good advice;
>   I'm looking you in the eye
>   and giving it to you straight:

"Don't be ornery like a horse or mule
   that needs bit and bridle
   to stay on track."

God-defiers are always in trouble;
   GOD-affirmers find themselves loved
   every time they turn around.

Celebrate GOD.
   Sing together—everyone!
   All you honest hearts, raise the roof!

THINK

- What does it mean to have a "fresh start" with God? How many times have you longed for that?
- What do you keep from God? Why do we do this when God knows us anyway? What prompts that kind of thinking?
- How does stubbornness keep us from God?
- When have you experienced God as your "island hideaway"? What does it take to get there?

PRAY

God, give me a fresh start . . .

READ God Lasts

Isaiah 40:26-31

Look at the night skies:
  Who do you think made all this?
Who marches this army of stars out each night,
  counts them off, calls each by name
—so magnificent! so powerful!—
  and never overlooks a single one?
Why would you ever complain, O Jacob,
  or, whine, Israel, saying,
"GOD has lost track of me.
  He doesn't care what happens to me"?
Don't you know anything? Haven't you been listening?
GOD doesn't come and go. God *lasts*.
  He's Creator of all you can see or imagine.
He doesn't get tired out, doesn't pause to catch his breath.
  And he knows *everything*, inside and out.
He energizes those who get tired,
  gives fresh strength to dropouts.
For even young people tire and drop out,
  young folk in their prime stumble and fall.
But those who wait upon GOD get fresh strength.
  They spread their wings and soar like eagles,
They run and don't get tired,
  they walk and don't lag behind.

THINK

- Describe times you felt God had abandoned you. What led to those feelings?
- How does God energize those who get tired? How has he energized you?
- What comfort is there in knowing that God doesn't come and go?

- How have you waited upon God in the past? What preceded that season in your life? How might you get there from where you are now?

PRAY

Lord, energize me . . .

LIVE

What I Want to Discuss

What have you discovered this week that you definitely want to discuss with your small group? Write that here. Then begin your small-group discussion with these thoughts.

So What?

Use the following space to summarize the truths you uncovered about your accomplishments and what you really need to do to move out of a "treading water" mindset. Review your "Beginning Place" if you need to remember where you began. How does God's truth impact the "next step" in your journey?

Then What?

What is one practical thing you can do to apply what you've discovered? Describe how you would put this into practice. What steps would you take? Remember to think realistically—an admirable but unreachable goal is as good as no goal. Discuss your goal in your small group to further define it.

How?

Identify how you will be held accountable to the goal you described. Who will be on your support team? What are their responsibilities? How will you measure the success of your plan? Write the details here.

MY
HAPPINESS

"I don't know how to have fun anymore."

A REMINDER:

Before you dive into this study, spend a little time reviewing what you wrote in the previous lesson's "Live" sections. How are you doing? Check with your small-group members and review your progress toward the specified goals. If necessary, adjust your goals and plans, and then recommit to them.

THE BEGINNING PLACE

"Life, liberty, and the pursuit of happiness." It's all right there in the Declaration of Independence. Is it any wonder why America is so focused on feeding or enticing the pleasure zone? Ask anyone what one thing they most desire in life and more often than not you'll hear an answer that sounds like this: "I just want to be happy."

Happiness. Fun. Enjoyment. Pleasure. All of these words tumble around in our lives like dollar bills in a windstorm. We reach for them, try to gather as many as we can, hoping that this next batch will last a little longer than the last. Even when we realize the transitory nature of happiness, we keep on grasping, arms flailing like an albatross in mating season.

Along the way, some of us forget how to have fun. Seriousness trumps frivolity, and life loses its tasty candy coating. Others of us neglect everything but the pursuit of fun. But men in both groups suddenly feel lost. Happiness dissipates or even disappears.

What about you? Where does your happiness come from? Do you still know how to have fun? Do you live only to have fun? What does it mean to enjoy life? Is that what God really wants for us?

Use the space below to summarize your beginning place for this lesson. Describe your reality as well as your dreams. We'll start here and then go deeper.

READ Forgetting Fun

From the *Minneapolis Star Tribune* article "Is This Fun or What?" by Rosalind Bentley[1]

The only things we know how to do naturally from the moment of birth are breathe, eat, sleep and go potty. Fun is a learned behavior—an art form, really.

Somewhere along the road to adulthood we lose our way, forget how to see sailboats and rose blossoms in cloud formations, and stop pretending that the bedcovers are a tent. We consider those pursuits immature. And if we have kids, we don't always join them when they do those things.

Or, we think you have to spend money to have fun. As such, we miss opportunities to connect with our loved ones in simple ways that take very little time.

From the *Knight Ridder/Tribune Media Services* article "A Good Childhood Is Not About the Trappings," by Debra-Lynn B. Hook[2]

A friend who is the mother of four grown children told me she once asked her adult children to recount their favorite memory of childhood. Was it the trip to Disney World or the time they rented a cottage at the beach? No, they said.

"It was riding around the living room on Daddy's back after supper."

THINK

- Do you agree that fun is a learned behavior? How is it learned?
- How would you rate your ability to have fun? How does that compare to when you were younger?
- List some of the things you would consider "fun." What does that list say about you?
- What would it take to improve your ability to enjoy life?

THINK (CONTINUED)

PRAY

Lord, show me how to enjoy . . .

READ The Pursuit of Happiness

Ecclesiastes 2:1-11

I said to myself, "Let's go for it—experiment with pleasure, have a good time!" But there was nothing to it, nothing but smoke.

What do I think of the fun-filled life? Insane! Inane!
    My verdict on the pursuit of happiness? Who needs it?
With the help of a bottle of wine
    and all the wisdom I could muster,
I tried my level best
    to penetrate the absurdity of life.
I wanted to get a handle on anything useful we mortals might do
    during the years we spend on this earth.

Oh, I did great things:
    built houses,
    planted vineyards,
    designed gardens and parks
        and planted a variety of fruit trees in them,
    made pools of water
        to irrigate the groves of trees.
I bought slaves, male and female,
        who had children, giving me even more slaves;
    then I acquired large herds and flocks,
        larger than any before me in Jerusalem.
I piled up silver and gold,
        loot from kings and kingdoms.
I gathered a chorus of singers to entertain me with song,
        and—most exquisite of all pleasures—
    voluptuous maidens for my bed.

Oh, how I prospered! I left all my predecessors in Jerusalem far behind, left them behind in the dust. What's more, I kept a clear head through it all. Everything I wanted I took—I never said no to myself. I gave in to every impulse, held back nothing. I sucked the marrow of pleasure out of every task—my reward to myself for a hard day's work!

Then I took a good look at everything I'd done, looked at all the sweat and hard work. But when I looked, I saw nothing but smoke. Smoke and spitting into the wind. There was nothing to any of it. Nothing.

THINK

- In what ways is this passage a picture of your life?
- What is the most difficult aspect of this picture for you to accept?
- When have you felt like the "fun-filled life" was insane? What led you to that conclusion?
- What does it look like to "suck the marrow of pleasure" in today's society? How have you attempted this?
- What do these verses imply about what's truly important in life?

PRAY

Father, lead me to what's important . . .

READ Even in Times of Peace . . .

From the *U.S. News & World Report* article "Happiness Explained," by Holly J. Morris[3]

Ahhh, happiness. Ineffable, elusive, and seemingly just out of reach. For most of the 20th century, happiness was largely viewed as denial or delusion. Psychologists were busy healing sick minds, not bettering healthy ones. Today, however, a growing body of psychologists is taking the mystery out of happiness and the search for the good life. . . .

Decades of studying depression have helped millions become less sad, but not necessarily more happy—a crucial distinction. When you alleviate depression (no mean task), "the best you can ever get to is zero," says [Martin] Seligman, a professor at the University of Pennsylvania. But "when you've got a nation in surplus and at peace and not in social turmoil," he explains, "I think the body politic lies awake at night thinking about 'How do I go from plus 2 to plus 8 in my life?'"

Indeed, people in peaceful, prosperous nations aren't necessarily getting any happier. Though census data show that many measures of quality of life have risen since World War II, the number of people who consider themselves happy remains flat. And people are 10 times as likely to suffer depression as those born two generations ago. Researchers have scads of information on what isn't making people happy. For example, once income provides basic needs, it doesn't correlate to happiness. Nor does intelligence, prestige, or sunny weather. People grow used to new climates, higher salaries, and better cars. Not only does the novelty fade but such changes do nothing to alleviate real problems—like that niggling fear that nobody likes you.

THINK

- Note that this article was published just before the events of 9/11. Considering this, what previous discoveries about the state of happiness surprise you most?
- How might the results of this kind of study be different today?
- What is your reaction to the claim that people are ten times as likely to suffer depression today than two generations ago?
- In what ways has depression affected your life?
- How much of your time do you spend trying to "not be unhappy" versus finding ways to increase your happiness?
- What do you correlate with happiness today? Is that a healthy view of happiness? Explain.

PRAY

God, grant me happiness . . .

READ No One Is *This* Happy

Philippians 4:10-14

I'm glad in God, far happier than you would ever guess—happy that you're again showing such strong concern for me. Not that you ever quit praying and thinking about me. You just had no chance to show it. Actually, I don't have a sense of needing anything personally. I've learned by now to be quite content whatever my circumstances. I'm just as happy with little as with much, with much as with little. I've found the recipe for being happy whether full or hungry, hands full or hands empty. Whatever I have, wherever I am, I can make it through anything in the One who makes me who I am. I don't mean that your help didn't mean a lot to me—it did. It was a beautiful thing that you came alongside me in my troubles.

Colossians 1:24-25

I want you to know how glad I am that it's me sitting here in this jail and not you. There's a lot of suffering to be entered into in this world—the kind of suffering Christ takes on. I welcome the chance to take my share in the church's part of that suffering. When I became a servant in this church, I experienced this suffering as a sheer gift, God's way of helping me serve you, laying out the whole truth.

THINK

- What allows Paul to see hardship as a good thing? (Or is he just trying to make his readers not feel bad about his situation?)
- If you were in Paul's situation as described in these verses, how happy would you be?
- Why is it so difficult to be content in all circumstances?
- When in your life have you felt like there was no chance of experiencing happiness?

- How in the world can suffering lead to happiness?
- If you could learn to view suffering and hardship as a gift from God, how would that change your everyday life?

PRAY

Lord, help me see suffering as . . .

READ If I Just Had More Money . . .

From the *Time* article "No Price Tag on Happiness," by Jeffrey Kluger[4]

Think that Porsche and boat and beach house you have been dreaming of would actually make you happy? Think again. Economist Richard Easterlin of the University of Southern California examined data from 1,500 people surveyed repeatedly over a 28-year period. He found that while healthy people are generally happier than unhealthy ones and married people are happier than unmarrieds, increases in wealth and material possessions improve happiness only briefly.

The reason is a pair of forces known as hedonic adaptation and social comparison. Translation: when you get something new, the thrill quickly wears off, and even if it didn't, there's always someone out there who has something better. The answer? Quit the money chase—or at least run more slowly—and devote more time to family, friends and home. These things, the study shows, really do pay higher returns in happiness.

From *The Treasure Principle*, by Randy Alcorn[5]

At the airport, Hugh Maclellan Jr. saw an acquaintance who looked troubled.

"What's the matter?" Hugh asked.

The man sighed. "I thought I was finally going to have a weekend to myself. But now I have to go supervise repairs on my house in Florida." Dejected, he sat waiting to take off in his private jet.

Here's a man with everything he needs, with what most people dream of; yet he couldn't even enjoy his weekend. He was enslaved by his possessions.

THINK

- What are examples in your life of seeking "stuff" or money in an attempt to be happy?

- How have you experienced "hedonic adaptation" or "social comparison"?
- If the thrill quickly wears off in the pursuit of happiness through stuff, why do people keep attempting this approach?
- When have you experienced the "higher returns" of happiness brought on by devotion to family, friends, and home?
- What specific actions could you take to reduce your reliance on money and stuff as the primary provider of happiness?

PRAY

God, give me balance in life by . . .

READ A Quiet Heart

Psalm 131:1-3

> GOD, I'm not trying to rule the roost,
>> I don't want to be king of the mountain.
> I haven't meddled where I have no business
>> or fantasized grandiose plans.
>
> I've kept my feet on the ground,
>> I've cultivated a quiet heart.
> Like a baby content in its mother's arms,
>> my soul is a baby content.
>
> Wait, Israel, for GOD. Wait with hope.
>> Hope now; hope always!

From *The Rabbi's Heartbeat*, by Brennan Manning[6]

Experience has taught me that I connect best with others when I connect with the core of myself. When I allow God to liberate me from unhealthy dependence on people, I listen more attentively, love more unselfishly, and am more compassionate and playful. I take myself less seriously, become aware that the breath of the Father is on my face and that my countenance is bright with laughter in the midst of an adventure that I thoroughly enjoy.

Conscientiously "wasting" time with God enables me to speak and act from greater strength, to forgive rather than nurse the latest bruise to my wounded ego, to be capable of magnanimity during the petty moments of life. It empowers me to lose myself, at least temporarily, against a greater background than the tableau of my fears and insecurities, to merely be still and know that God is God.

As a fringe benefit, practicing silent solitude enables us to sleep less and feel more energetic. The energy expended in the impostor's exhausting pursuit of illusory happiness is now available to be focused on the things that really matter—love, friendship, and intimacy with God. The "still, small voice" is what you need to hear.

THINK

- In what ways do you strive to be "king of the mountain"?
- What are the components of a faith life that keeps your "feet on the ground"?
- Describe times when you've cultivated a quiet heart. How did you do this?
- When have you "wasted time with God"? How does time spent with God in silence affect your level of contentedness?
- What is "the impostor's exhausting pursuit of illusory happiness"? In what ways have you pursued the illusion of happiness?
- What deliberate steps would you need to take to cultivate a quiet heart? How might that give you hope?

PRAY

Lord, help me take steps to . . .

READ The Road to Happiness?

Matthew 5:1-12

When Jesus saw his ministry drawing huge crowds, he climbed a hillside. Those who were apprenticed to him, the committed, climbed with him. Arriving at a quiet place, he sat down and taught his climbing companions. This is what he said:

"You're blessed when you're at the end of your rope. With less of you there is more of God and his rule.

"You're blessed when you feel you've lost what is most dear to you. Only then can you be embraced by the One most dear to you.

"You're blessed when you're content with just who you are—no more, no less. That's the moment you find yourselves proud owners of everything that can't be bought.

"You're blessed when you've worked up a good appetite for God. He's food and drink in the best meal you'll ever eat.

"You're blessed when you care. At the moment of being 'careful,' you find yourselves cared for.

"You're blessed when you get your inside world—your mind and heart—put right. Then you can see God in the outside world.

"You're blessed when you can show people how to cooperate instead of compete or fight. That's when you discover who you really are, and your place in God's family.

"You're blessed when your commitment to God provokes persecution. The persecution drives you even deeper into God's kingdom.

"Not only that—count yourselves blessed every time people put you down or throw you out or speak lies about you to discredit me. What it means is that the truth is too close for comfort and they are uncomfortable. You can be glad when that happens—give a cheer, even!—for though they don't like it, I do! And all heaven applauds. And know that you are in good company. My prophets and witnesses have always gotten into this kind of trouble.

THINK

- What implications does Jesus' message have for the concept of "happiness"?
- How have you experienced the blessedness that Jesus talks about?
- In what ways is this passage a backward way of thinking about what leads to happiness?
- Think about when you've been "at the end of your rope." Did you feel blessed in that experience? If not, how could you have?
- What does it mean to "work up a good appetite for God"? Describe practical ways you can do that and how that can bring you happiness.

PRAY

Father, put me on the path to . . .

LIVE

What I Want to Discuss

What have you discovered this week that you definitely want to discuss with your small group? Write that here. Then begin your small-group discussion with these thoughts.

So What?

Use the following space to summarize the truths you uncovered about your accomplishments and what you really need to do to move out of a "treading water" mindset. Review your "Beginning Place" if you need to remember where you began. How does God's truth impact the "next step" in your journey?

Then What?

What is one practical thing you can do to apply what you've discovered? Describe how you would put this into practice. What steps would you take? Remember to think realistically—an admirable but unreachable goal is as good as no goal. Discuss your goal in your small group to further define it.

How?

Identify how you will be held accountable to the goal you described. Who will be on your support team? What are their responsibilities? How will you measure the success of your plan? Write the details here.

HOPE

"No more 'smoke and spitting into the wind.'"

A TIME TO REVIEW

We come to the final lesson in our *Treading Water in an Empty Pool* discussion guide, but this is not an ending place. Hopefully, you've been discovering some truths about your life and seen opportunity for change—positive change. But no matter what has brought you to lesson 8, know that this is merely a pause in your journey.

You may have uncovered behaviors or thoughts that demanded change. Perhaps you've already changed them. Will the changes stick? How will you continue to take the momentum from this study into next week, next month, and next year? Use this lesson as a time to not only review what you discovered but also determine how you'll stay on track tomorrow.

Talk about your plans with small-group members, commit your plans to prayer, and then do what you say you'll do. As you move forward with a renewed sense of purpose, you'll shrink desperation and grow hope.

READ Your Job

Colossians 3:22-25

Servants, do what you're told by your earthly masters. And don't just do the minimum that will get you by. Do your best. Work from the heart for your real Master, for God, confident that you'll get paid in full when you come into your inheritance. Keep in mind always that the ultimate Master you're serving is Christ. The sullen servant who does shoddy work will be held responsible. Being Christian doesn't cover up bad work.

THINK

- What hopes and dreams do you have for your job?
- What "greater goal" might God have for you in your current job situation?

PRAY

Lord, show me . . .

LIVE

- How does God's truth impact the "next step" in your journey?
- How will you get there?
- How will you be held accountable?

READ Your Accomplishments

Job 12:13-16

> True wisdom and real power belong to God;
>> from him we learn how to live,
>> and also what to live for.
> If he tears something down, it's down for good;
>> if he locks people up, they're locked up for good.
> If he holds back the rain, there's a drought;
>> if he lets it loose, there's a flood.
> Strength and success belong to God;
>> both deceived and deceiver must answer to him.

THINK

- From unmet goals, what can you learn that will help you with future accomplishments?
- What faith-related goal can you strive for? What is the Holy Spirit's role in helping you reach this goal?

PRAY

God, encourage me . . .

LIVE

- How does God's truth impact the "next step" in your journey?
- How will you get there?
- How will you be held accountable?

READ Your Friends

Ecclesiastes 4:9-10

> It's better to have a partner than go it alone.
> Share the work, share the wealth.
> And if one falls down, the other helps,
> But if there's no one to help, tough!

THINK

- What is the greatest challenge facing you regarding friendships?
- How can your faith help you overcome that challenge, allow you to be a good friend, and help you develop good friendships?

PRAY

Father, guide me . . .

LIVE

- How does God's truth impact the "next step" in your journey?
- How will you get there?
- How will you be held accountable?

READ Your Children

Isaiah 58:7

> What I'm interested in seeing you do is:
>> sharing your food with the hungry,
>> inviting the homeless poor into your homes,
>> putting clothes on the shivering ill-clad,
>> being available to your own families.

THINK

- What aspect of parenting is the most problematic for you?
- What truths from the Bible can help you as you work through that problem?

PRAY

God, help me . . .

LIVE

- How does God's truth impact the "next step" in your journey?
- How will you get there?
- How will you be held accountable?

READ Your Wife

Ephesians 5:25-28

Husbands, go all out in your love for your wives, exactly as Christ did for the church—a love marked by giving, not getting. Christ's love makes the church whole. His words evoke her beauty. Everything he does and says is designed to bring the best out of her, dressing her in dazzling white silk, radiant with holiness. And that is how husbands ought to love their wives. They're really doing themselves a favor—since they're already "one" in marriage.

THINK

- In what ways is your relationship with your wife less than it could be?
- With the guidance of the Holy Spirit, how might you improve that relationship?

PRAY

Lord, counsel me . . .

LIVE

- How does God's truth impact the "next step" in your journey?
- How will you get there?
- How will you be held accountable?

READ Your Faith

Isaiah 40:28

> Don't you know anything? Haven't you been listening?
> GOD doesn't come and go. God lasts.
>> He's Creator of all you can see or imagine.
> He doesn't get tired out, doesn't pause to catch his breath.
>> And he knows everything, inside and out.

THINK

- How does the faith you live out today compare with the faith you lived when you first became a Christian?
- In what ways can you "wait upon God"? How will that energize your faith?

PRAY

God, change me . . .

LIVE

- How does God's truth impact the "next step" in your journey?
- How will you get there?
- How will you be held accountable?

READ   Your Happiness

Psalm 131:2

> I've kept my feet on the ground,
>   I've cultivated a quiet heart.
> Like a baby content in its mother's arms,
>   my soul is a baby content.

THINK

- In what specific ways have you made "happiness" a goal in your life? How have you tried to reach that goal?
- Where does contentedness come from and how can you get there?

PRAY

Father, illuminate me . . .

LIVE

- How does God's truth impact the "next step" in your journey?
- How will you get there?
- How will you be held accountable?

NOTES

LESSON 1

1. From *Death of a Salesman,* by Arthur Miller, copyright © 1949, renewed 1977 by Arthur Miller. Used by permission of Viking Penguin, a division of Penguin Group (USA) Inc.
2. "Lesson One: Job Stuff," *Fast Company* (November 1999).
3. Brian Dumaine, "Why Do We Work?" *Fortune: Investor's 1995 Guide* (December 26, 1994). © 1995 TIME Inc. All rights reserved.
4. Sondra Farrell Bazrod, "Finding Meaning, Happiness in Your Work," *Health Services Network* (December 2, 2001).

LESSON 2

1. John F. Kennedy, "Special Message to the Congress on Urgent National Needs," (May 25, 1961).
2. Jerry White, *Dangers Men Face: Overcoming the Five Greatest Threats to Living Life Well* (Colorado Springs, Colo.: NavPress, 1997), pp. 22-23.
3. Michael S. Malone, "Money and the Meaning of Life," *Fast Company* (June 1, 1997).
4. Excerpted from *The Treasure Principle,* © 2001 by Eternal Perspective Ministries. Used by permission of Multnomah Publishers.

LESSON 3

1. Les and Leslie Parrott, "Why Friends Fail," ChristianityToday.com (December 2002).
2. Excerpt from p. 58 of *The Four Loves,* copyright © 1960 by C. S. Lewis, renewed 1988 by Arthur Owen Barfield, reprinted by permission of Harcourt, Inc.
3. "Don't Underestimate the Value of Friends," *Wisconsin State Journal* (July 15, 2000).
4. Parrott.

LESSON 4

1. Glenn T. Stanton, *My Crazy Imperfect Christian Family: Living Out Your Faith with Those Who Know You Best* (Colorado Springs, Colo.: NavPress, 2004), pp. 128-129.
2. "The Daddy Dividend," *Psychology Today* (March 1, 2002). Reprinted with permission from *Psychology Today* magazine. Copyright © 2003 by Sussex Publishers, Inc.
3. Gary Rosberg, *Guard Your Heart* (Sisters, Ore.: Multnomah, 1994).

LESSON 5

1. Copyright The Good News Broadcasting Association, Inc. From a written transcript of a *Gateway to Joy* radio program (August 13, 2001).
2. Donald Margulies, *Dinner with Friends*, pp. 85-86. © 2000 by Donald Margulies. Reprinted with the permission of Theater Communications Group.
3. Michele Weiner Davis, *The Sex-Starved Marriage: A Couple's Guide to Boosting Their Marriage Libido* (New York: Simon & Schuster, 2003), pp. 3-4, 8. Reprinted with the permission of Simon & Schuster Adult Publishing Group. Copyright © 2003 by Michele Weiner-Davis.
4. Steve Tracy, "What Does the Bible Say?" MarriagePartnership.com.
5. Excerpts from pp. 91, 114-115 of *The Four Loves*, copyright © 1960 by C. S. Lewis, renewed 1988 by Arthur Owen Barfield, reprinted by permission of Harcourt, Inc.
6. Karen S. Peterson, "Infidelity Reaches Beyond Having Sex," *USA Today*. Copyright © January 9, 2003. Reprinted with permission.

LESSON 6

1. Bill Thrall, Bruce McNicol, and John Lynch, *TrueFaced: Trust God and Others with Who You Really Are* (Colorado Springs, Colo.: NavPress, 2004), pp. 46-47.
2. Jerry Bridges, *The Pursuit of Holiness* (Colorado Springs, Colo.: NavPress, 2003), pp. 109-110.

LESSON 7

1. Rosalind Bentley, "Is This Fun or What?" *Minneapolis Star Tribune*.
2. Debra-Lynn B. Hook, "A Good Childhood Is Not About the Trappings," copyright 2004, Knight Ridder/Tribune Media Services. Reprinted with permission.
3. Copyright 2001, *U.S. News & World Report*, L. P. Reprinted with permission.
4. © 2003 TIME Inc. Reprinted by permission.
5. Excerpted from *The Treasure Principle*, © 2001 by Eternal Perspective Ministries. Used by permission of Multnomah Publishers.
6. Brennan Manning, *The Rabbi's Heartbeat* (Colorado Springs, Colo.: NavPress, 2003), pp. 43-44.

ANOTHER "PULL-NO-PUNCHES" HONEST DIALOGUE ABOUT THE ISSUES THAT MATTER MOST TO MEN.

Leaning into a Hail of Bullets

Men face a maelstrom of temptation every hour of every day. As deep as readers dare to go, this study is a venue for small-group participants and individuals to take on the temptations that threaten their lives. Relevant and practical, this study is easy to use and will lead you and other men to dive into these heart issues—as deep as you dare to go.

The Navigators
1-57683-690-8

Perfect companion to the REAL LIFE STUFF FOR MEN series.

The Message

All sixty-six books of the *Message* Bible are conveniently combined into one. From the mysterious Old Testament stories to the straightforward teachings of Jesus to the encouraging early church letters, reading *The Message* will jump-start your heart, challenge your mind, and forever change your life.

Eugene H. Peterson
1-57683-289-9

To order copies, visit your local Christian bookstore,
call NavPress at 1-800-366-7788,
or log on to www.navpress.com.

To locate a Christian bookstore near you,
call 1-800-991-7747.

BRINGING TRUTH TO LIFE
www.navpress.com